NIGHTMARE ALLEY . . .

The scream was terrifying. The sound you might expect to hear from someone falling into the fires of hell. Bennett stopped and listened. It had happened so suddenly he wasn't able to identify where the scream had come from. He heard it again, this time cut off midway, abruptly ended. It had come from the alley he'd just left. He turned back and ran, gun drawn.

The alley was ominously silent. He slowed to a walk, proceeding with great caution, wishing he had a flashlight that would let him see into the dark corners. Nothing seemed changed from a few minutes before. Except in the area behind the warehouse. There, a section of boxes and cartons that he remembered as having been piled up against the rear of the building had fallen and were now scattered on the pavement. He walked slowly toward them.

Just as he saw the body lying behind one of the larger cartons, he was attacked once again. This time the killer leaped at him from behind, knocking him to his knees. He saw the knife blade flash in the light from the distant street lamp as he fell. He tried to roll when he hit the pavement, to avoid the slashing sweep of the knife. He managed to hold onto his gun, although the back of his right hand was painfully scraped against the asphalt.

His attacker crouched above, left hand raised and holding the knife, right hand against Bennett's throat. Bennett moved just as the killer's left hand slashed toward him. The knife barely missed his throat and caught in the shoulder of his jacket, cutting the material as easily as if it had been snow.

The killer, like a furious animal, drove the knife toward Bennett again and again. . . .

The Bennett Series:

BENNETT'S WORLD

1

It was called detached service and Bennett had been on it so long he'd nearly forgotten what it was like to attend roll calls or wear a clean, pressed uniform. He hadn't been to headquarters since the assignment had begun, and at the rate things were going, he didn't see himself reporting there in the near or distant future. Somehow he'd become a cop who wore dirty clothes and could be taken for a street bum.

The dimly lighted clock in the window of the pawn shop across the street read 2:55. By day the avenue was bumper to bumper with traffic. At this time of night a car occasionally sped by, or a city bus passed, heading west on the half hour and east on the hour; otherwise the street was deserted. Bennett slouched in the dark doorway of an empty store, occupants long gone while the owner tried to raise enough capital to tear down the building and erect anything that would give him a better return on his money. The area smelled of urine and vomit and all the lousy odors that pollute the air on the skid rows of large cities. Los Angeles was no different from any other, even though handsome, famous Hollywood was only a fifteen-minute bus ride away.

A slowly moving car was approaching, headlights on high beam. In the sudden light Bennett saw his reflection in the empty store window: a down-at-the-heels drunk, filthy, clothes ragged and worn, an ideal candidate for a mugger or a pickpocket. Or even a murderer, which was the reason he froze his ass off every night, play-acting drunk and senseless to entice into killing him whoever it was who had been slitting throats in this sad part of the city.

The passing car was a taxi, and in the back seat a man and a woman were locked in passionate embrace. From the cab's slow erratic path, Bennett guessed that the driver was paying more attention to his rearview mirror than to the road.

Once the cab had gone the doorway was again dark as pitch. Bennett cautiously shifted his weight. His left foot ached and he wiggled it inside his shoe, trying to restore circulation to his cramped and freezing toes. He knew if it didn't get better he'd have to stand and pound his foot on the pavement—hardly the movement of a benumbed drunk.

He heard the sound before he saw anything. What might have been a cautiously placed foot, in the alley that adjoined the deserted store. Bennett kept his eyes closed and waited. The city rumbled in the distance, even at this late hour. Far away a piece of emergency equipment wailed in the night. A single siren. Police or ambulance, not fire. Fire equipment was a wailing and tooting orchestra, Klaxons burping like gorillas, sirens singing to other following sirens. Bennett lay still and held the city's noises at their distant perspective while waiting for the single closer sound he knew would come again.

He opened his eyes a slit, keeping his head out of the light so there would be no reflection from the street

2

lamp in front of the pawnshop. He saw nothing. Then, although there was no breeze to cause it, a shadow at the alley corner of the building moved slightly. Because he had shifted his leg to stop the uncomfortable tingling, he was no longer in a position to quickly roll left or right. If that shadow was cast by someone with a knife he would be on top of Bennett before he could get to his feet. He lay still. If he moved he might frighten away whoever it was, and he'd waited too long for this moment.

The shadow moved again. After what seemed to be an interminable time, the uneven line now assumed the vague shape of a body standing erect, poised as if to attack. Bennett continued breathing slowly and laboriously—a drunk who had consumed three times the alcohol he could manage, lying exposed and vulnerable in a foul-smelling doorway, waiting, unsuspecting, to have his throat sliced open.

The lights from a municipal bus brightened the street. The bus was heading east, which meant it was the hour, straight up, three o'clock in the morning. The shadow froze in the safety of the alley, where the headlights could not pick it out. The shadow knew its way around, it knew how to find protection from bus headlights; hug the west wall of a building on the hour, and hug the east wall on the half-hour.

The bus stopped at the corner just beyond where Bennett lay and discharged a passenger, then moved on, leaving behind a thin trail of black smoke that hovered in the air a moment before it lazily settled to the pavement. The man who'd gotten off the bus hurried down the side street, his steps echoing nervously.

Then it was quiet. Bennett continued his ragged deep breathing, fluttering his lip occasionally in imitation of a snore. He moved his toes again, and felt the

3

instep of his left foot begin to cramp. If he had been at home asleep it would have awakened him and he would have jumped out of bed and stamped the foot on the carpet with all his strength, as though he had stepped on a loose rattlesnake and didn't dare release his hold until the creature was dead. It would have awakened Polly and she would have turned on the light and asked if he was all right, hoping he hadn't had another of his Vietnam nightmares, where he was back in the jungle in the black of night waiting with pounding heart for the moment when a screaming gook would leap upon him.

Before he realized what was happening someone was upon him and someone's weight had shoved him back against the locked store door. The street light picked out the blade of a glimmering knife. It was poised above Bennett, and before he could move it plunged toward his throat. He rolled aside, kicking himself away from his attacker by jamming his feet against the store window and shoving as hard as he could. The slashing knife missed his throat and he felt the tip catch the sleeve of his jacket. He now saw his attacker, dressed in man's clothes, all black, pants and shoes and high-necked sweater. A black knit watch-cap was pulled low over a face covered with a mannequin's mask, a mask with porcelain-like skin, eyebrows coquettishly arched over open holes through which Bennett could see mad eyes. The mask's nose and lips were delicately and perfectly formed, the mouth enticingly open, desirable lips slightly parted. Bennett tried to grab for the mask, to rip it off and identify his assailant, but the knife slashed at him again and he had to use both hands to try to escape the blade.

Another siren began wailing, this one closer and approaching. Bennett tried to roll out of the doorway as

4

he yanked at his attacker's knife-holding arm. Once they were in the street there was the chance that a passerby would see them and call for help.

Suddenly Bennett was alone. He was lying half in the doorway and half on the pavement, the back of his head sore from where it had hit the door. The attacker had rushed away and was gone. Bennett listened for departing footsteps and heard nothing. *Rubber-soled shoes*, he thought.

He had his police special in his fist as he darted around the corner of the empty store. He saw nothing. He walked slowly down the dark alley, weapon in hand, trusting his peripheral vision to detect movement on either side of him. The approaching siren had stopped three or four blocks away. He couldn't radio for help because he'd refused a walkie-talkie. Any damn fool could see he was carrying the damn thing, he had told Drang; it would tip off his possible assailant to stay clear of him, which was exactly the opposite of what he wanted to happen.

Halfway down the alley he stopped at the rear of a warehouse. Stacked against the side of the building were cardboard boxes ranging in size from man's shirt to home refrigerator-freezer combination. Heavy iron grilles barred the windows, as they did every building in the alley. He saw no one.

Cautiously, he continued to the next cross-street without seeing anyone. Sidewalks and street were deserted. He debated whether or not he'd frightened away the assailant and decided he probably had. He shoved his gun back in the shoulder holster he wore under the grimy shirt sweater and jacket he'd put on to keep out the cold, all the while grateful that, since it was November, he was working this miserable night shift in Southern California and not New York or Chicago, where his steamy breath would balloon from him as he walked back up the alley. He had parked his car in a lot two blocks from where he had huddled in the doorway. He made himself walk slowly and unevenly, stopped several times and swayed drunkenly. Until he was clear of this place he had to look like a person who belonged on these dismal streets at this awful hour, a likely victim for someone the newspapers and radio and television stations were calling the mad killer.

The scream was terrifying. The sound you might expect to hear from someone falling into the fires of hell. Bennett stopped and listened. It had happened so suddenly he wasn't able to identify where the scream had come from. He heard it again, this time cut off midway, abruptly ended. It had come from the alley he'd just left. He turned back and ran, gun drawn.

The alley was ominously silent. He slowed to a walk, proceeding with great caution, wishing he had a flashlight that would let him see into the dark corners of each building he passed. Nothing seemed changed from a few minutes before. Except in the area behind the warehouse. There, a section of boxes and cartons that he remembered as having been piled against the rear of the building had fallen and were now scattered on the pavement. He walked slowly toward them. Just as he saw the body lying behind one of the larger cartons, he was attacked once again. This time the killer leaped at him from behind, knocking him to his knees. He saw the knife blade flash in the light from the distant street lamp as he fell. He tried to roll when he hit the pavement, to avoid the slashing sweep of the knife. He managed to hold onto his gun, although the back of his right hand was painfully scraped against the asphalt. His attacker, still wearing the porcelain mask, crouched above Bennett, left hand raised and holding the knife, right hand against Bennett's throat. Bennett, who'd landed on his right side when he'd stopped rolling, jerked his body to free his right hand, which held his gun and was under him. He moved just as the killer's left hand slashed toward him. The knife barely missed his throat and caught in the shoulder of his jacket, cutting the material as easily as if it had been snow. The killer, like a furious animal, drove the knife toward Bennett again and again, while Bennett frantically used all his strength to fend off the blade.

He finally freed his right arm by rolling onto his back. He raised the gun and fired directly at his target, who hovered above him, the porcelain mask staring down without emotion. The knife slashed at Bennett's hand as he fired, deflecting his aim. Then with surprising speed the killer ran away, his rubber-soled black shoes making no sound. Bennett fired a second shot from a kneeling position, using both hands to insure his aim, but the killer ran a zig-zag pattern and disappeared between two buildings. Bennett raced down the alley in pursuit, but his assailant was gone.

Back at the warehouse Bennett found the body of a middle-aged man, his throat slit, the puddled blood warm. The victim was dressed in old dirty clothes, needed a shave and a haircut, and probably could have used a bath, from the dirt on his hands. Bennett found a pay phone, called the precinct, and reported the murder without identifying himself. Then, because he wanted to stay on the case, he disappeared before the police arrived. He watched the black-and-whites drive up and the officers rope off the area. He saw the homicide men and the medical examiner's men and the evidence crew arrive and had the certain feeling that if the person guilty of this murder and those that had preceded it was going to be caught, he, Frederick Bennett, would be the one who made the arrest, not any member of the mixed crew who scurried around the body lying like a pile of rejected clothing alongside an empty washing-machine carton.

He left the area when the coroner's van arrived. He expected that Drang would be hovering around, and a block away from the alley he saw Drang's four-door blue Dodge parked near a sad-looking all-night restaurant. He waited until a passing car had disappeared in the distance before opening the passenger door and sliding in beside his boss, Detective Captain Rufus Drang, immaculate as ever in slacks and sports jacket.

"What the hell happened?" Drang asked.

"I wish you'd greet people before leaping at them," Bennett said.

Drang ran a tan well-manicured hand through his close-cropped graying hair. "You've been out here on the street . . . how long?" he asked.

"Two and a half weeks," Bennett said.

"Two and a half weeks," Drang echoed, "and not only have you not come up with anything, there's a killing right under your goddam nose."

It was unlike Drang. The two men had graduated from the academy together, had been on the force for ten years, and although Drang was Bennett's superior, their relationship had always been on an equal, one-to-one level.

"Who's pressuring you?" Bennett asked.

Drang ran his hand through his hair once again. "Everybody," he confessed. "Newspapers, television stations, even a goddam radio station is calling for action, streets not safe to walk in, that crap. So of course the chief is on the horn yelling, and the Board of Supervisors lets it be known they're unhappy even if it's out of their bailiwick and none of their goddam business. And every half-assed politician in the county from city councilman to a spokesperson for the Rapid Transit District is making a speech, and they all dump on me." He looked at Bennett in the dim light and saw the cuts in the jacket. "What the hell happened?" he asked.

"I got jumped."

"Could you identify him?" Drang asked.

"Slight, could be a man or a woman, very strong, agile, wearing black clothing, including a watch-cap pulled low. And a mask."

"Mask?"

Bennett described the mask, the porcelain surface, the pert nose, lips half smiling, half open invitingly, brows arched over open holes. "And inside you could see the eyes of whoever it was. Dark, I think, dark blue, or brown, or black, I couldn't tell."

"I think I've seen those masks someplace," Drang said.

"In department stores," Bennett said. "In the cosmetic department, usually. They're decorative. I never thought of them as being worn by anyone."

"How's Polly holding up?" Drang asked, a question out of the blue.

"She's doing all right," Bennett replied. "Why'd you ask?"

Drang shrugged modestly. "I have an interest in the health and welfare of the men I work with and of their families," he said by way of explanation. "Nothing more than that."

"God, it's miserable down here," Bennett said. "These poor bastards, they're camped on the edge of life, and somebody's pushing them off." He shuddered and rubbed the back of his right hand. The skin had

9

been scraped from it as if he'd used sand paper. Drang saw the red flesh.

"How'd that happen?" he asked.

Bennett told him in more detail of the fight he'd had with the killer. "Mad as a hatter," he concluded. "Whoever it is."

Drang agreed.

Bennett yawned and stretched. "Well, nice to have seen you," he said. "Always a pleasure talking to one of the city's finest. I'm going to sniff around for awhile." He opened the car door.

"Take it easy," Drang cautioned.

Bennett waved his right hand in agreement and ducked quickly out of sight. If anyone was watching, he didn't want himself connected with Drang or the unmarked Dodge. After the car had driven away Bennett entered the all-night restaurant. It was brightly lit, with a U-shaped counter in the center and a few tables against the walls on either side. A grill was in the center of the U, and an elderly man in a dirty white chef's outfit leaned against it, drinking coffee out of a brown mug. Beside him was a counter surface where sandwiches were made up. No one else was in the place. Plastic flowers were stuck into plastic glasses on each table and in four selected spots on the counter. Neon and hand-lettered soft drink and beer signs were strategically placed on the back wall. Bennett sat on a stool in the center of the U before a paper napkin dispenser, salt and pepper shakers, a glass cup filled with sugar, a bottle of catsup, and a nearly empty jar of mustard the color of dried molasses.

The old man looked at Bennett suspiciously, at the scraped right hand, the torn dirty jacket, the unshaven face and uncombed black hair. He didn't say what'll you have or good evening or anything else. He stayed

10

where he was, the small of his back against the grill, his right hand not too far from a chef's knife that lay near an open loaf of sliced white bread.

"Coffee," Bennett said.

"It's a quarter," the old man said without moving.

Bennett dug into his trouser pocket and made much of fishing around for money. As he did this he complained. "A quarter? Jesus H. Christ, just because you're the only joint that's still open you sure as hell take liberties with your customer's finances."

The old man shrugged that he didn't much care about his customer's finances.

Bennett found a quarter and laid it on the counter. The old man examined it to make sure it was an American coin, that it wasn't bent or otherwise mutilated, in fact did everything but place it between his teeth and bite on it, and then grabbed an off-white cup and saucer from a shelf under the coffeemaker and poured thick stale coffee out of a Silex.

"Black," Bennett said.

The old man filled the cup and placed it in front of Bennett.

"Spoon," Bennett said. Before the old man could ask why he added, "I use sugar."

The old man reached under the counter. He came up with a soup spoon. "We're out of regular coffee spoons," he explained.

"Busy night?" Bennett asked.

The old man's face formed and reformed into a series of expressions whose purpose was to brag that the place had been jammed with people all the night long until just a few seconds ago.

Bennett put sugar into the coffee and stirred. The sound filled the small cafe, metal banging against cheap crockery. "You hear the sirens?" Bennett asked.

11

"Sirens?" The old man retreated, pressing against the grill.

Bennett gestured toward the alley a block away. "Cops, everything. Even the coroner's wagon. Dead guy in the alley." He sipped at what was the worst cup of coffee he'd ever tasted. "Throat cut from here to here." Spoon in hand, he traced the path across his neck. "I got the hell out of there."

The old man's eyes were wide with fright. "You shitting me?" he asked, his reedy voice tremulous.

"About the guy in the alley?" Bennett asked. "Hell no."

The old man sucked in his breath. "Who done it?" he asked after he'd found his voice again.

"Who the hell knows?" Bennett said. "You ever hear of anything like that? Somebody's walking around loose who should be in a cage, right?"

"Oh yeah," the old man breathed.

"Beats me," Bennett said woefully. "Why'd anyone want to kill an old bum? Guy was about your age," he told the old man. "I saw him," he continued. "I walked over to see what all those cops were doing and I saw him before they put a sheet over him. About your age, with his throat cut from here to here." He illustrated with the spoon once again. "Real mess," he said, and sipped at the dreadful coffee.

"My God," the old man's voice whistled noisily.

"I was going to meet my buddy over there, and then the cops arrived so I left the place," Bennett said.

"Is that your buddy that you were talking to?" the old man wanted to know.

"I was talking to?" Bennett repeated.

"Outside," the chef said. "Before you come in here you was sitting in a car with a guy talking. Who was you talking to?"

"Beats the hell out of me," Bennett said quickly. *I have to tell Drang not to park in front of an open business,* he thought. "This guy he yelled at me when I was going to come in here. He wanted to know what had happened back there. He heard the sirens and saw all the cops' cars and he wanted to know what the hell had happened. I told him. Scared the bejesus out of him and he drove the hell away from here." He sipped more coffee and tried to swallow the thick sticky stuff without gagging.

"Oh yeah," the old man said. He seemed satisfied with the answer. "I think I seen the guy around here before is why I asked," he said.

"I never saw him before," Bennett said. "You think maybe he's queer? You think that was maybe why he wanted me to get into his car with him?" Bennett asked.

"Wouldn't be the first time," the old man said.

"Well, why didn't I think of that before?" Bennett wondered. "Can you imagine that?"

"The world's full of them," the old man sagely advised.

"I suppose so," Bennett conceded, wondering what Drang's opinion of this conversation would be.

"The guy who was killed," the old man began. "Do you know who he was?"

"His name, you mean? No, I didn't hear anybody give him a name. Why, you missing someone?"

"I know a lot of the guys," the old man said. "I spent a couple of years out there, on and off, before I got myself settled here." He looked for some wood and knocked on it. In the harsh cafe light thousands of tiny red veins mottled his face like a rash. "A lot of them guys, they're good old boys. They didn't do nothing to nobody. Like you. I bet you, you just got dealt a couple of bad hands. True or false?"

Bennett wrinkled his forehead and rubbed his nose with the back of his left hand, the unharmed hand. "Well, that's true. I'd have to say that's true."

"See?" the old man said, complimenting himself. "I could tell. Not at first," he hastened to add. "But after you was here awhile I could tell. Hell, when you first come in I didn't know what you were. You can understand that," he said.

"Oh yeah," Bennett agreed. "Hey," he said. "Maybe you know my buddy? The one I was going to meet? Little guy, but strong as a goddam horse. Always wears black. Black shoes, black pants, black sweater, black watch-cap. You know him?"

The old man thought about it. "He got a name?" he asked.

"Wouldn't ever give it to anybody. You know how some guys are."

The old man agreed he knew how some guys were.

"He been in here?" Bennett asked, trying to keep the conversation from drifting with the old man's disconnected thoughts.

"Your buddy?" the old man asked.

"Right," Bennett said. "I was supposed to meet him and then everything got screwed up when the cops arrived. He been in here?"

"Not's I remember," the old man said, scratching his neck below his left ear. "There's been people in tonight, but I don't recall anyone like you describe."

"Did you ever see him?" Bennett asked, chatting pleasantly. "Hell of a guy."

"I don't think I ever seen him," the old man said. "He always in black?"

"Most of the time," Bennett said. "Little guy," he

14

repeated, holding his hand parallel to the floor to illustrate his assailant's height. "Strong as a horse. Funny guy," he concluded, snorting wryly. "Funny as a son of a bitch."

"No, he was never in here," the old man said. Then, thoughtfully, "Little guy?" he asked, frowning. "Black watch-cap like in the navy?"

"Yeah. Right."

"I seen him once," the old man said. "He was out there, in front of the joint, walking. Back and forth. Like he was waiting for somebody."

"Tonight?" Bennett asked.

"No, it wasn't tonight. I don't think it was tonight." He scratched his neck again. "Not tonight."

"When was it?" Bennett asked. After he'd said it he realized he was pushing too hard.

The old man's expression changed. He'd warmed up to Bennett during their conversation. Now, suddenly, his face went blank. He leaned back and folded his scrimpy old arms across his chest and stared just past Bennett's left ear. Then he shrugged, his answer to Bennett's question.

Bennett swallowed the last of his coffee. "Well," he said, "I suppose if I hang around back there he'll find me. If he drifts in, tell him where I went, okay?" Without waiting for a reply he moved to the door and opened it. "Nice to have seen you," he said, and stepped out into the street.

15

2

Detective Captain Rufus Drang stood at the side of the alley as the coroner's men lifted the sheet-covered body, slung it on a gurney, and pushed the load on its silent rubber wheels to the rear of their van. They lifted it, shoved it inside, then murmured good-byes to detectives, cops, medical-examiner personnel, and evidence men and drove off, the sudden starting of their motor an abrupt punctuation in the night.

Drang was wondering if he'd been right, bending the rules as he had, by allowing Bennett to work detached service without a partner, without any backup, even a radio to signal for help if he got into trouble. In Drang's opinion, Bennett had just barely gotten himself out of a nearly fatal spot tonight, a pigeon lying in a dirty alley, enticement for a killer. It wouldn't have gone as far if there had been someone covering him, another officer just out of sight but listening on an open radio for the sounds of trouble. They might have caught whoever it was who got kicks out of slaughtering lost men.

Camera flashes lighted the alley as the evidence crew photographed the spot where the body had been found, a place where dark blood, quickly drying, stained an

16

area already marked with oil and grease and urine and vomit. A big-city alley. *What a place to die,* Drang thought.

"Captain?"

One of his homicide men had called. Drang walked to where the man stood, between the rear of the warehouse building and the place where the body had been found.

"Here's where he was hiding," the officer said. His name was Arthur Dennis. He was in his early thirties, a friendly, unassuming man no one would identify as a homicide officer. He pointed to a small area between the rear wall of the building and the stack of boxes. "All the rest of this junk is piled against the building," he said. "He pushed these aside and made a neat little goddam cave for himself."

Drang stepped into what might have been a child's hiding place in a game of hide-and-seek. Whoever it was had concealed himself here after carefully moving stacks of boxes out from the wall, then replacing everything, leaving a peephole through which he could look from one end of the alley to the other. Hidden here, you could see your victim. There was no way your victim could see you.

"He saw the guy coming, waited until he got right there—" Dennis pointed to the area where the body had lain—"and jumped him. Poor bastard never knew what hit him."

"See if he dropped anything," Drang said, moving away.

Drang tried to picture some poor bum staggering through the alley, perhaps looking for a place to sleep and, seeing the stacked cartons, moving toward them. Then, so suddenly the bum's addled brain couldn't re-

17

alize what was happening, the killer had stepped from his hiding place and used his knife. A single great slash, ear to ear, from behind, probably, holding the victim by his hair. Then quickly step back and let the poor bastard fall, his life running out onto the alley pavement in gushing streams, the way blood spurts when one of the great arteries has been cut.

Drang hurried back to Dennis. "There might be sheets of plastic or stacks of old newspapers stuck into these cartons. Go through everything," he ordered.

When he turned away he saw that several of the people who frequented the area had gathered behind the police ropes to stare at the place where one of them had been killed. Among them stood Bennett. Drang gestured with his head and walked down the alley toward the next cross-street. Bennett joined him in a doorway under a fire escape so rusted it seemed about to collapse.

"The only covering I saw was the mask," Bennett said.

"How'd he keep the blood off his clothes?" Drang wondered.

"You may be right about the plastic," Bennett conceded. "But I doubt it. I think down here, in these alleys, he strips off his outer clothes after he's done his job, dumps them in any of those trash containers, and scoots. You think he's gone for the night?"

"Yes. Why don't you get the hell out of here? You got some sort of fascination for this place?" Drang asked as if they stood in the center of a garbage dump. "When's the last time you were home?"

"Couple of nights ago," Bennett said, starting to move. "Yeah, I think I'll get cleaned up and start fresh tomorrow."

"Fred?"

18

Bennett waited.

"I know you want to do this without a backup, but they damn near got you tonight."

Bennett shrugged. "Goes with the territory," he said.

"That's pretty stupid," Drang said angrily. "We're talking about taking unnecessary chances, not selling shoes door to door. You've put yourself in a position where what happened here tonight could happen to you."

"It won't," Bennett said reassuringly. "Come on, Drang, you know I'm not bucking for hero. I take care of myself very well. But there's a cuckoo loose down here who's pushing people over the edge and it's our sworn duty to put a stop to it. There's a certain risk involved in that, of course." Whenever Bennett preached about the duties of the police officer he spoke in a sardonic tone that infuriated the Captain. "But that's the name of the game, after all. We move in and put our money where our mouths are, so to speak. There are risks involved, as you've pointed out. No question about it, but it's our sworn duty. . . ."

"Shut up," Drang said.

Bennett did.

Drang's blue eyes were hard as steel. "You're a bastard," he said.

"Now Captain," Bennett protested. "You know that's not true. You're just upset because of all this killing that's been going on. And that's what we're going to stop, Captain. Shall we continue as before?"

Drang looked as if there might be a new murderer in town, with Bennett his victim. Bennett grinned. "I won't get killed," he said softly. "Take my word."

Drang didn't reply. He turned quickly and stomped back up the alley. Midway he stopped to kick a trash can, which clattered loudly. Bennett walked away in the opposite direction, to the lot where he'd left his car. When he'd made sure no one was watching, he drove off.

It was still dark when he pulled into the driveway of the valley house he and Polly had bought when they'd first married, eight years before, when Bennett had been on the force less than a year. He'd come home from Vietnam shaken and so emotionally bruised that the Army doctors who'd examined him thought it was highly unlikely he'd ever again be able to function normally. He was not afraid of physical hurt, never had been—but the daily death count wore at his nervous system, a day-by-day reminder of his own losses when he was a child. He'd served courageously, dutifully stealing into the jungle on the search-and-destroy missions that were his primary assignment. It had all ended on a scream that last awful day, when he'd cracked wide and they'd taken him back to the hospital. There was nothing more he was willing to do or able to do or capable of doing, so they sent him home and dumped him in a hospital where he was talked to and lectured at and sympathized with and eventually he surprised everyone by beginning to function. He listened to and advised others; he visited with his stepfather and made plans about what he might do with his future; he even accepted passes that allowed him to leave the hospital grounds and go into town for an hour or so. Next he was given weekend passes, and met and talked to people on the outside, people who didn't know or especially care about Vietnam or his place in it. For the most part the trauma was buried, pushed back from his conscious mind so that he functioned, on the surface at least, as well as the next fellow. He had occasional periods of relapse, where something would trigger him back to Vietnam, back amidst the horrors, back among men like himself who were screaming or crying or bravely striding one minute, and the next were unrecognizable bits and pieces of flesh and bone and blood and muscle.

Bennett had been there once when that happened. He and Len Gordon had been moving cautiously through tall grass and trees when Len had stepped on a mine. He'd known what he'd done and had stopped dead still.

"Oh Jesus God," he'd said.

Bennett had halted with him.

"It's going to explode as soon as I lift my weight off it," Len had said, barely breathing, his voice a hoarse whisper, as though if he spoke normally it would change the pressure on the mine and the device would blow anyone nearby to kingdom come.

"I'll find something," Bennett had said, "something your exact weight and we'll make the exchange, I'll put it on the mine and you'll step off."

"Bullshit," Len Gordon had said. "That's pure bull-shit, Freddie. You get the hell back, get back behind that tree before this thing blows. There's no reason we both have to get it."

Bennett had hesitated, not wanting to leave the best friend he'd ever had.

"Get the hell out of here," Len Gordon had yelled.

And Bennett had turned and run for cover. He had stopped to look back just at the instant Len stepped off the mine. It all happened at once. Bennett screamed and the mine blew Len Gordon into bits and pieces and a hunk of muscle or bone popped into Bennett's open mouth.

There wasn't enough of Len Gordon left to bury,

and there wasn't enough of Bennett left to be of any use to the United States Army. Since he was screaming so damn much they airlifted him back to base camp and the hospital.

Sometimes, even now, ten or more years later, he woke up tasting blood and bone. The last known remains of Len Gordon.

He pressed the garage-door opener and waited for the door to rise and clear the way. He pulled in beside Polly's car, crawled out of his, and unlocked and opened the door between the garage and the house. He and Polly had painted and papered and disguised the place so efficiently and imaginatively that it was hard to identify this lovely home as the tract house they'd bought. Bennett, of course, had done only what Polly had specifically asked him to do. He had little interest in a home, except as a place where he ate some of his meals and slept most of the time.

"Fred?" Polly called from the bedroom, turning on a lamp.

"It's me, hon," he answered.

He opened the refrigerator, looking for something to eat or drink. He had half a loaf of bread, the remains of a roast chicken, and a can of beer in his hands when she appeared.

"I didn't want to wake you," he explained, setting the food on the counter.

She was about to embrace him when she saw the back of his right hand.

"What's that? What happened?" She sounded more angry than concerned.

"What? Oh, you mean this?" He flashed the hand for an instant, then held it so she wasn't able to examine it.

"Let me see that," she ordered. When he didn't change position or do what she'd asked, she said, "Fred!" angrily.

He showed her his hand. "I scraped it," he said, hoping that would explain it away.

"How?"

"On the pavement."

"And what were you doing on the pavement?"

"Come on, hon," he said softly. "We don't want to go into those things."

"Because they're ugly?" she asked him. "Like your work is ugly?"

He put his arms around her and pressed his face against her lustrous blonde hair, which she'd braided for sleep. "Now come on hon," he said quietly. "You don't mean that. It's not ugly, it's just damn hard." She shook her head, as if she wanted to say something but had changed her mind. Then, "Maybe we should face that," she said. "If it's damn hard for you, maybe we should sit down and talk about it. Maybe if it's damn hard we should talk about you doing something else." She drew back, stepped out of his embrace, and stared into his hard black eyes. "Should we do that?"

They stood an arm's length from one another, each one waiting to see what the other was going to do or say.

He broke the frieze. He rubbed his scraped hand against his cheek, then grinned tiredly.

"Whatever it is we decide, we'll do it together. But I'm too exhausted right this minute to come to any what-I'm-going-to-do-with-my-life decisions." He looked wearily at the kitchen window. A subtle shading had begun outside. What had been velvet black had become a deep iron gray beyond which hovered the suspicion of red.

23

"What time is it?" he asked her.

"Five-thirty," she said. "I'll fix you something to eat. Sit down."

"Let me wash up first," he said. "Polly?"

She'd turned away from him and was slicing the cold chicken. "Hm?" she said without looking at him.

"We will talk this out, but not when I'm beat," he said.

"Do you know how many times you've told me that?" she asked him. "Can you remember how many times you've assured me that we'd talk this over when you weren't so beat?" She slammed down the knife and faced him. "Can you understand that when you're gone from here, working—especially since you've gotten into this detached service nonsense—that while you're gone I'm terrified for you? Doesn't that get to you?"

"Of course it gets to me," he said, trying to keep his voice even, trying not to shout at her, trying not to be as stubborn as he knew he could be. "Jesus, Polly, I know how you worry about me, I can see it in your face. I try to reassure you that I'm all right, but you won't listen. You knew what the work was when we got married. We talked about this when we first got married."

"But I didn't realize you'd have this kind of duty. I thought you'd be more of an administrator. I thought by now your ambitions would have led you toward what Rufus does, not what you've been doing."

"Well, how about that," he said, scratching his head. "Well if that doesn't knock the hell out of a conversation. Drang wants to be head *jefe*," he explained. "I have no interest in that. He can lead the band, star in the play, do whatever the hell he wants that keeps him all neat and clean without a goddam scrape on the back of his right hand. He can stay manicured and

24

neatly shaved forever. It doesn't have anything to do with me because that's not me, that's not the way I'm put together. I have to get in among them. You know that. You told me once that's what you loved about me, that I wasn't afraid of life. You appreciated that I can't stand by and watch: I'm incapable of being a voyeur as far as life is concerned. I have to jump in with everyone else. I'd make a lousy king, but Drang could probably handle it. If he wasn't able to do it he'd fake it, he'd vamp until he learned what the next move was. I can't do that. I've tried, but I can't." He was running out of words. His throat felt dry, and his eyes burned with exhaustion. "But there are a couple of things I can do," he said quietly. "I can love you more than anything in the world, and I can take care of myself. This?" he held out the hand. "If I'd had any brains I'd have cleaned it up before I came home, so it wouldn't look so lousy. But I just wanted to get home."

"I know all that," she said. She touched his cheek with her hand. "And when I said that's why I loved you I was telling you the truth." She leaned forward and kissed him. "Now wash up and eat something and get some sleep."

He was too tired to do more than nibble at his food. He showered before getting into bed and was asleep the minute he stretched out. He didn't sleep peacefully. He dreamed about porcelain masks that came alive, cheeks blowing in and out, eyes winking, mouths pursed for a kiss or a whistle, he couldn't be sure which; and then he was walking along a street piled with dirty snow on one side, while the other was sunny and warm. Porcelain-faced men and women lived on both sides of this remarkable avenue. Suddenly, as though provoked, everyone crossed to the warm side, where Bennett stood, and approached him menacingly. He could see now that the masks were really the faces of Orientals who were dressed in the loose, pajama-like clothing the natives had worn in Vietnam. They were armed, some with rifles, others with carbines or automatic pistols. One tossed a hand grenade into the air and caught it, the way a boy plays with a ball. He heard a sound, a sharp sound, and the figures froze into position, as though an invisible substance had been released and had paralyzed everyone on the street. Before Bennett's horrified eyes the porcelain faces began to crack, fine lines fracturing into wide fissures. He heard the noise once again and wasn't able to identify it. He looked for his weapon, searched his pockets, groped for a rifle sling, tried to find a holster on his body. Meanwhile the porcelain masks began to leak blood through the crevices, as though only red blood was behind the porcelain.

"Fred?"

One of the shattered masks was trying to speak.

"Fred?"

For a moment he didn't know where he was. Polly had pulled shut the bedroom drapes and the room was dark. He saw her standing beside the bed. His first reaction, before he recognized her, was to pull away.

"Fred? Telephone. It's Rufus. He said to wake you. He said it was important."

"What time . . . ?" His voice sounded far-away in his ears, as though someone else had spoken the words.

"Just noon. Do you want to talk to him? I'll bring you the phone."

"Yeah. Please."

She brought it in, the long white cord trailing like a domesticated worm, and placed it on the bed beside him. He took the receiver from her.

"Yeah," he said, his voice controlled. "What's up?"

"Radio station KRFM just broadcast a message from our killer," Drang said. "They've sent a copy of the tape over to us."

"What's the message?"

"You want the whole thing?" Drang asked. "It's fourteen minutes long."

"No, not the whole thing. The heart of it."

"He tells a long, involved tale about the crappy conditions on earth and how people are suffering and then he goes into his place in the world and how he has therefore been affected——"

Bennett interrupted. "You keep saying 'he,'" he said. "Is it a man?"

"I think so, although the voice is very light and slightly sibilant. It might be a woman, but I doubt it."

"I do too."

"He finally gets to the murders, and explains how it's a holy cause, his words, and he's cleansing the world of trash, of what he called detritus—leftovers I take him to mean, unnecessaries—and there's a long diatribe about that, about how some people don't fit and are like an albatross around humanity's neck and what a great thing this is he's doing and he's sore as hell about how his good work is being misunderstood with the media calling him names like 'killer' and 'monster' and so on."

"Does he say anything about when it'll all end? When he'll be finished with this crusade?" Bennett wanted to know.

"Not directly, no," Drang said. "But if you read between his lines, there is no end. He may have to clean everyone off the planet until he's all that's left, the only really decent guy in all creation."

Polly came into the room with a mug of coffee. Ben-

27

nett silently thanked her and sipped the hot liquid. "Well, we've got our work cut out for us," he told Drang, "if it's his plan to slaughter everyone on earth."

"I'm detaching three more officers to join you down there," Drang said. "We'll give him some more targets."

"You'll have more cops than bums roaming the street," Bennett said.

"I'll get you a transcript of the tape," Drang said.

"I'll be down there by five," Bennett said, and hung up.

"What happened?" Polly asked.

"Local radio station received a tape made by a sickie who claims to be the killer. Drang was giving me the highlights."

"And you think he'll slaughter everyone on earth?" she asked. "Is that what you said?" Polly's reaction to fear or frustration was anger, and now she was angry. Her face was white, her hands clenched and unclenched, her slender body was tight as a bow.

"Hey," Bennett cautioned quietly, "we said we weren't going to get into that."

"How can we avoid it?" she demanded in a fury. "How the hell can we not discuss the fact that under the best of conditions you're doing extremely dangerous work. And that now the conditions aren't the best, they're the worst, and you're the department's pigeon. You don't seem to understand that you're not just doing something awful to yourself, you're doing it to me. Damn it!" She slammed one fist into her open palm. *"Damn it!"* she repeated.

Bennett reached out his hand. "Sit down," he said. "Sit here for a minute. It's not all that bad."

She hesitated, face turned away from him.

28

"Pol?" he said.

"Oh, dammit!" she cried. She sat beside him on the edge of the bed. "I'm so scared," she said. "I don't want it to rub off on you, but I'm so scared."

He pulled her to him and held her. "It's going to be all right," he said, trying to reassure her. "Swear to God, Pol, it's going to be all right."

Usually, when she was frightened, this would calm her, his comforting words and cool voice would allay her fears. But more and more, her normal condition had become a state of terror. She found herself living in a nightmare world where what she waited for and had grown to expect was word that something awful had happened to him: he'd been hurt, he was blinded, he was paralyzed, he was dead. When he was away her nerves jumped at odd moments, so that, unable to control herself, she would spill a cup of coffee, or drop a magazine, or suddenly feel that she was going to cry, or even scream.

"Fred?" she said through her tears. "You know I love you. But I'm not sure I can handle it any more. I try. Honest to God I try. But I'm not sure I can handle it any more. And if I can't . . ." she had to stop. She wasn't able to say it. "If I can't," she made herself continue, "then I don't know if I can stay married to you."

She'd never before said it aloud. It was something they'd avoided talking about, something they'd spoken around, but never directly faced.

"Do you understand?" she asked him.

"Well, it's nothing we can't solve," he told her, not able to accept what she'd said. "There's a solution to everything."

She pulled away from him. "No," she angrily said. "There's not a solution to everything. The difficulties

29

we're having are a case in point. I've looked and looked and I haven't figured out a solution."

His throat was dry. He was going to say, "Now Pol," and hold her in his arms again but he knew that wouldn't do any good. So he just nodded his head, forced to agree that whatever was wrong in their marriage wouldn't be easy to repair.

3

Bennett parked his car near the downtown railroad terminal at about four o'clock. He was supposed to meet Drang in an Olvera Street restaurant called El Rey. He was unable to clear his mind of the conversation with Polly. It hadn't been necessary for her to tell him how she felt about their marriage; he'd known, but hadn't been able to admit it to himself. He'd hoped that something miraculous would happen that would allow her to share his dangerous profession with him, and so enrich their relationship, but he'd known it wasn't working out that way. Polly had been completely honest when she'd said she couldn't take it anymore. What made him tremble with anxiety was the fact that he didn't know what to do about it.

El Rey was a small restaurant in the center of Olvera Street, a wide promenade of well-tended basket and pottery and candle shops for the tourist trade. Bennett recognized two fellow officers mingling with the crowd—Charlie Simpson, an older man with thinning gray hair above a sharp, sad face whose mournful eyes, the lids hanging at the outer corners, gave him a hangdog appearance that was helpful to the dangerous

31

job at hand; and Tom White, a husky young black man in worn Army fatigues, whose right hand nervously rubbed against his nose. Bennett let them precede him into El Rey, waiting beside an outer stall that sold the souvenirs you bring home to help you remember where you've been. Ashtrays, pillows, T-shirts, baseball caps, and pieces of fake red rock, all bearing inscriptions: Welcome to L.A., Greetings from Hollywood, or simply Olvera Street, Los Angeles, California.

As he was about to enter the restaurant he saw, on the opposite side of the street, a figure dressed all in black, its back to him, looking into the window of a shop that sold ceremonial masks, Mexican-Indian masks of sun gods and fertility gods and harvest gods.

"Hey, Bennett?"

The voice was behind him. Bennett turned to see another police officer, this one a young man, freckled, red haired, and green eyed. Sean MacManus was dressed for a night's work in torn jeans, worn boots, and a filthy plastic raincoat.

"You going in?" he asked.

Bennett turned back to the mask shop. The slight figure dressed in black was gone. Bennett searched the crowded street, but saw no sign of it.

"Yeah, let's go, Sean," he said, and they walked into El Rey together.

A record was playing on the jukebox as they entered the bar area, which was just inside the entrance to the left of a small lobby where stood a short, portly gentleman in tuxedo trousers, a frilled white shirt, and a maroon cummerbund.

"Holy Mother of God," this man said when he saw Bennett. "You look terrible."

"*Buenos dias*, Miguel," Bennett said.

32

"Not *dias, tardes*," Miguel said. Then he made a clucking sound, as if Bennett were a child who'd made a mistake. "Spanish is not your mother tongue," he said. "Not even your cousin-once-removed tongue."

Bennett shrugged. "What do I get for the try?"

"A hundred points," Miguel said. "Drang's in there," he nodded toward a shut door on which a sign read, "No Admittance. Employees Only."

MacManus followed Bennett through the bar. They opened the door without knocking and entered a small office–storage room. Drang was seated behind a battered old desk, Charlie Simpson and Tom White on stacked cartons that, judging from their stamped labels, contained cans of salsa and jars of olives.

"Sit anywhere," Drang said. Behind him could be seen an alley through which deliveries were made to the shops and restaurants this side of the street. Bennett sat on a low stool normally used to reach the top of the shelves that lined one wall and held canned goods and boxes of rice, sauces, cheeses, and a gallimaufry of cans and bottles and boxes. Sean MacManus lowered himself to the floor, his back to the wall, and his feet, crossed at the ankles, stretched out into the room.

"Bennett will be in charge of the unit," Drang said. "If you spot the guy, contact Bennett. Don't take unnecessary chances, but don't put yourself in a position where you're not a target for him. Understood?"

They all agreed they understood.

Drang turned to Bennett. "How are you going to maintain contact?" he asked.

"Visual," Bennett said. "I don't want to use radios. They're bulky, you have to talk into them, and if they're to be of any use they'd be on so you could receive—and that's more likely to scare him away than help us catch him. That all right with you guys?"

Tom White nodded with the others, then asked, "By visual you mean one man always sees one man?"

"Right," Bennett agreed. "I'll take one end and be in visual contact with you, you maintain visual contact with me and Sean, Sean with you and Charlie, Charlie with Sean."

"You and me are the two ends," Charlie Simpson said.

"Right," Bennett agreed. "Unless you'd rather one of the other guys took that end."

"Who looks more like a bum than me?" Charlie asked. "My wife used to call my eyes soulful. Now she thinks I should go to a plastic surgeon and have him take all this stuff away she used to think was soulful." He ruefully tugged at the corners of his eyes. "I might have to do it anyway to improve my peripheral vision."

"Soulful?" Sean asked incredulously. "She really thought that? She was putting you on."

"Probably," Charlie agreed. "Because if I'm soulful she's the only person in the world who ever noticed it."

Drang leaned forward, very much the leader, muscular arms resting on the desk top. He looked at Bennett, whose knees, because the stool on which he sat was so low, nearly touched his chin. "What do you think?" he asked. "Will you get him?"

"I think so. Yeah," Bennett said. "He's got to do something wrong soon. I think he already has—we just haven't spotted it. We've got an assortment of targets for him." He looked around at the others. "And once we're on the street we all look helpless, which is what he likes." He squinted his eyes. "Why is it most killers are bullies?" he asked the room.

No one answered.

Drang stood and waited while the others unwound from where they'd been seated. "Let's get to work," he told them. "Good luck." He strode from the room very much the man in charge.

When he'd gone Bennett gave position assignments. "That's for tonight," he said. "No one moves more than a block, one way or the other. You should look drunk and helpless enough not to be able to navigate any further than that. If he attacks, grab him and identify yourself. Use your weapons only if you have to. If we bring in a dead man, somebody's going to accuse us of covering the thing up by killing a ringer just to save the department's neck."

He told them of his experience the night before, and described the man and the mask. "And he's strong," he added. "Wiry and strong as hell. He had me down and for a while I couldn't get away from him. He's also very quick." He looked at the others and recognized the tension they felt. *It's like going into battle,* he thought. The enemy is out there and he's waiting to kill you. It doesn't really matter whether it's one man or a hundred. Someone is out there who wants you dead. For an instant he had sympathy for Polly, and realized how she must feel at home alone, trying to guess what was happening to him. He wondered, if the positions were reversed, whether he'd be able to wait each day for Polly to come home, fearful that she might not, that it had happened—that someone in the dark had gotten to her.

Someone in the dark. Out in the city, someone in the dark was waiting, hunting, stalking. *My God, I might as well be back in Vietnam,* he thought as he and the others left the room. Another record was on the

35

jukebox, a recording of "La Virgen de la Macarena," the trumpet announcing the entrance of the toreadors. Miguel stood erect beside the machine, trying to suck in his round belly so that the charging bull wouldn't tear out his guts with its sharp horn.

"*Buenas tardes*, Miguel," Bennett said.

"Damn near *noches*," Miguel replied."

"Yeah, well," Bennett agreed.

It was nearly night outside. The sun had disappeared and to the west newly erected skyscrapers were silhouetted against a reddening sky. The city was emptying of its daytime population as workers boarded buses or drove cars out of parking garages toward already crowded freeways. The men separated as soon as they were outside the restaurant, becoming lonely individuals aimlessly drifting. Bennett didn't immediately follow them. He walked back across the street to the mask shop and looked through the glass, searching for the sort of porcelain mask his assailant had been wearing the night before. None was in the window and he entered the shop. A pretty young woman with dark hair, a fresh flower behind her ear, greeted him with something less than enthusiasm.

"Can I help you?" she asked doubtfully, looking at his unshaven face and uncombed hair, his torn shirt and stained trousers.

"I'm looking for a mask," Bennett told her. "It's made of porcelain, I think. At least it looks like porcelain. You know the kind I mean?"

She smiled politely. "Porcelain?" she asked. "We carry Indian masks, tribal masks from the Northwest and from Central and South America. None of them are made of porcelain." She waited for him to excuse himself and leave.

"The one I want is made of porcelain," he said stub-

36

bornly. "It's French, perhaps that's the best way to describe it. Like a French-made mask that might be worn at a court function. Elegant. Fine eyebrows, eyeholes for the wearer, a perfectly shaped mouth, lips rosy. Have you any idea where I could get something like that?"

She stared at him as if he were mad. "I've never heard of that sort of mask," she said. "I can't imagine what civilization would have developed such a thing, or what its purpose would be."

"Well, I'm not concerned about the civilization," he said. "I'd just sort of like to get a mask like that. For the little woman," he added. "Something she can wear to masked balls. We go to three or four a year."

Suddenly the young woman's face lit up. If she'd been a cartoon a balloon would have appeared over her head with the single word "Eureka!" written on it. "No no," she said, "not a mask. That's not a mask. That's a decorator's design piece. They're made for retail stores as decorative pieces."

"Where would I get one?"

"At any store where they're used," she said. "I'm sure they'd be happy to sell you one. Or tell you where you could buy one. Will there be anything else?"

"No, thank you for your time," Bennett said. "You've been very helpful."

As he started to leave she had a further thought. "Of course," she said, "that's also the sort of item a person could make for himself. A potter, for instance—he'd have the equipment."

This was just the sort of information Bennett didn't want. "That opens the territory," he said. "Thanks."

Outside he threaded his way through the crowds who'd come to sightsee, to buy gifts, or to dine.

37

Families with young children in tow, little ones riding on fathers' shoulders, safe above the crowd, with a better view of the action than anyone else there. Small children looking with excitement and wonder at a variety of toys and dolls and colorful playthings exhibited in open-front shops. No one paid any attention to Bennett; drifters were a part of the street population.

He made his way to his station, a block that had once been a smart shopping area and now needed a wrecking crew to tear down sagging buildings so that clean new structures could be built to attract new businesses and renew the area. The streets were littered with old newspapers and discarded handbills that hawked cheap hotels or advertised the money to be made by selling a pint of blood. Held up together they made a kind of awful sense; sell a pint of blood for enough money to pay for a couple of nights in a hotel that might not be classy but was warm and dry and had beds that were a hell of a lot softer than the pavement in an alley or a deserted store front.

Bennett settled down on his haunches at the entrance to the first alley on the street he would police. Opposite him was the hotel whose handbills he'd seen, the Royal it was called, the name stenciled across a torn awning that covered the entry, and repeated vertically on a sign that extended the full five stories, from roof to first floor. A few room air-conditioners extended from the building out of quarters where the tenants, unable to bear the noise and smell of the street on especially hot nights and days, needed to shut their windows. The other rooms facing the street had blinds drawn or windows open, limp gray curtains drifting out like ghosts too ill to escape. The rest of the opposite side of the street was made up of deserted stores, a square two-story pile that had been an office building or small factory, a small bar whose flashing neon sign had just been turned on and read "Eats—Drinks," and at the far corner a parking lot, now nearly empty of cars.

Bennett's side of the street was not much different. Empty stores, a deserted movie theater, and a building that had probably been a warehouse and was now boarded up.

He could see Tom White at the far corner, walking slowly past the parking lot, to all eyes a disreputable black man down on his luck, grubbing for enough money to buy a bottle of cheap wine, which he'd drink in the privacy of an alley like the one in which Bennett huddled. Bennett couldn't see the others. White was his visual contact. The city's lights were on, the sky painting heavy black over the last sliver of blue, a mournful cover for the ugly streets the men patrolled.

Bennett wondered, hunched down against a dirty brick wall, what sort of person they were trying to catch. Who would kill at random in this fashion? What sort of person would stalk a man made helpless by alcohol, attack someone who wasn't aware he was being attacked until the last moment, when it was too late, when the knife blade touched his throat and sliced in, cut flesh and tendons, reached the artery and released the pulsating blood. A sickie, they'd all agreed. But wasn't anyone who murdered sick? Wasn't it insane to try to solve a problem by killing? They were talking about degree, Bennett guessed. The difference was between murder in the second degree—where the crime is a result of a sudden emotional swing that excludes reason or good sense in an explosion of pure passion—and murder in the first degree—where the crime is planned, plotted, and the victim is stalked, set in place as though he were a duck. *A sitting duck*, Bennett thought, *like the four of us*. If the killer knows we're after him, then here we are, sitting ducks, set out for a crazy to kill.

After half an hour of hunkering against the brick wall, Bennett rose and walked slowly toward the far corner. As he moved, a block away Tom White walked away from Bennett toward his next far corner, and Bennett knew each man would be doing the same, enlarging the territory, covering more ground where the killer might be. Bennett stopped at a trash can on the street beside the empty theater and pushed the contents from side to side. If the killer was watching, Bennett was a street bum looking for something he could sell. Tom White was out of sight for a moment; he'd slid into an alley in the middle of his block. Bennett left the trash can and continued his aimless walk toward the corner. He stood there scratching himself, ready to move quickly if he heard a yell or a gunshot, then saw Tom White step out of the alley and continue toward his far corner.

They continued their pattern without incident until after midnight. By then Bennett and the others were bored, chilled, and hungry, which meant this was the most dangerous time for them; they were not as alert as they had to be to survive. Bennett was mulling over whether they should spell each other and grab a cup of coffee and a sandwich when he saw an elderly man approaching, arms swinging, erect as a soldier, dressed in what had been a uniform at one time, from the looks of it. He stopped in a motion so military Bennett half expected heels to click. What at a distance had looked like a uniform were really well-cut khaki pants and a jacket of military cut, both worn but clean. On the man's face was a benign expression of love, and his pale eyes were moist behind thick glasses. His face was angular and lined, deep furrows cutting from each nostril to his chin, so his thin-lipped mouth appeared to be a bridge between two towers.

"Have you renounced evil?" he asked in a reedy voice. "Have you told the Lord God of your faults and your sins? If you were to die now are you prepared to meet your Maker?"

"I'm all right, thanks for your thoughts," Bennett said, turning away.

The old man scooted around so he once again faced Bennett. "You are not ready," he said. "Nor do I think you have prepared yourself to be ready. Why else would a young man like you be on mean and filthy streets? Have you a family?"

"Oh, yes. Really, everything's in good shape," Bennett said. "One thing we must all remember. Things are not what they seem."

"Oh, but they are," the old man corrected him. "Perception without understanding leads us to believe things are not what they seem. Perception with understanding allows us to know things are precisely what we perceive them to be. In you I see a fellow creature in dire trouble. A man allowing himself to be destroyed. It's not too late to discover who you are. With Divine help you can return to a productive role in society. No longer need you crawl among the filth. No longer need you beg or steal. No longer need you live this unnatural life."

"Well, thanks," Bennett said. "That cheers me up."

The old man plunged his hand into his jacket pocket and pulled out a small printed card, which he held between his fingers as if he were a magician about to perform a trick.

41

"This card will bring you peace now and forever," he said. "Follow the instructions on this card and you will never again find yourself in the sad state you are now in." His fingers moved swiftly and the card was held out for Bennett to take.

"Prayer. Action. Good Thoughts and Deeds." was printed on one side. On the other it said: "Carlisle Mountain Genesee. Man of God. Man of the People."

"Thank you, sir," Bennett said. "I'm sure you've helped many poor souls on these streets."

"Oh, yes," Carlisle Mountain Genesee replied.

"I know of one who desperately needs attention," Bennett said. "Even more than me. A slight man, dressed in black, wearing a black watch-cap. I saw him yesterday. I haven't seen him since. It seemed to me he was sorely in need."

The old man closed his eyes, held his hands together as if in prayer, and repeated Bennett's brief description of the killer. "A slight man, dressed all in black, and wearing a black watch-cap."

"Yes. Do you know him? He needs help badly."

"Sonny," the old man said. "You've described Sonny."

"You know him?"

"I have helped Sonny," the old man said. "Sonny has begun the journey to decent living and a wholesome life." He peered at Bennett over his clasped hands. "How do you know Sonny?" he asked. He sounded puzzled, as though knowing Sonny was an experience limited to a chosen few and he couldn't understand how a man like Bennett had become a member of such a group.

"Here and there," Bennett said. "The way you know someone on the street. You meet them here and there."

The old man seemed satisfied with the explanation.

"You have any idea where he is now?" Bennett asked.

"Why?"

"Just curious," Bennett said. "I haven't seen him since yesterday and I wondered if he was all right. The way things are down here . . ." he shuddered and put his hand to his throat protectively. "Could happen to any of us. Have you seen him today? Is he all right?"

"I saw him earlier this evening," the old man said. "He was strong and healthy, and we spoke, and he assured me that he has begun to change his life, that he will no longer waste his life on these streets. As you are doing," he concluded, pale, moist eyes fastening on Bennett accusingly.

"Where did you see him?" Bennett asked.

"Outside the chili place, next door to the Majestic," the old man said, his hand waving behind him and to his right.

"Do you meet him there often?" Bennett asked.

The old man smiled slightly, cracking the deep lines on either side of his mouth. "When it is necessary for me to see him, we meet," he said. "Divine guidance leads us to meet. If I am needed I will be there. I was needed here tonight, and I am here beside you. Whether you accept my message at this moment is something I cannot control. You will eventually accept my message because you must. The choice is not yours, although it might seem to be. The choice is made elsewhere. And since man is Divine he will accept the choice, and no longer live his life in these streets, but will accept the Lord and be led from hell." He blinked his eyes to clear them of tears.

Bennett felt a great surge of sympathy for this man,

43

who so desperately tried to help the poorest of the poor, whose beliefs were so simple and direct, whose answers to life's most difficult and complex problems were so uncomplicated and straightforward. Believe in God and He will lead you from these streets.

And then what? Bennett thought. *You're off the streets and then what?* He remembered J. D. saying to him, when he was a small boy not doing his chores, "You got to make the effort. There's no such thing as a free lunch. Remember, son, God only helps those that help themselves." Bennett wanted to repeat it to the old man, but there was no need to. Carlisle Mountain Genesee's belief got him through the night and that's about all you could expect for your dollar. Get through the night. Face the new day with fresh wind and a continuing belief that if you struggled and pushed and shoved and smiled and did everything humanly possible to survive you could make it through another day and another night.

Polly had softened his bitter views, his hard feelings, his merciless outlook. When he fell in love with Polly the world lost its hard edges, the sharp corners and steep inclines became passable, and you could get from here to there, from morning to night, without self-destructing. Polly had shown him the way to the good life and in return he was showing her the way to agony, to fear and hurt. Did he love her enough to help her? Or would he insist she live her life his way?

"Please," the old man said. "Change your way of living. God will accept you and help you. Just believe in Him. Trust Him. Surely it will be better than this." His hand moved beseechingly.

"What's Sonny's last name?" Bennett asked.

"Sonny, just Sonny," the old man said. "What an odd name for a grown man."

44

Bennett agreed that it was.

"So many lost sheep," the old man said. "Such a long journey to tend them all."

"Did you know the ones who were killed?" Bennett asked.

"I know everyone on the street," the old man said. "It's a poor flock, to some eyes, but with God's help we will survive. We will prevail." Again his eyes were misty, and he removed his thick glasses and blotted his tears before they escaped, using a tattered handkerchief he pulled from his inner pocket. He returned the handkerchief, replaced his eyeglasses, and cleared his throat, the sound rasping against the silence. "You asked if I'd known the others, those who are gone. Yes. I knew them."

"Did you know them well?" Bennett asked.

"Well?" The old man considered the question. "We pass, and touch for a moment. We don't know each other well. We appear and disappear, for the sea is large. All at the end is memory. Images cavort in our memory." He stopped to listen to himself. "Those poor men," he said, very softly. "Those poor men. What terrible waste."

Bennett was struck by the man's openness. It was as if he were witness to a confession. For a moment it seemed the old man would tell Bennett the most private thoughts about himself and the people he knew.

But Carlisle Mountain Genesee had said enough. He drew himself erect, shoulders back, stomach tucked in, made a smart military about-face and strode away, his steps in tempo with a holy march only he heard. Bennett watched until he'd reached the far corner and turned into a cross-street. Then he was gone.

Bennett strode toward White, who'd observed all this from his block.

"Who was that?" White asked.

Bennett told him. "He gave me our man's name. It's Sonny. He said he saw Sonny earlier tonight over near the Majestic. Take care of the unit, I'm going hunting."

"Take care," White said. "He damn near got you last time."

4

If at two o'clock in the morning you were feeling blue, the lobby of the Majestic hotel was a place where you might go to convince yourself that suicide was your only answer. When first built the Majestic had been an upper-middle-class hotel full to capacity because it was located in the center of the downtown business district. The original carpet, furniture, and wall decorations were still there. The furniture was shabby genteel, heavy brocade upholstery stained by years of wear from guests who'd sat and stared at other guests. The carpet had been thick, muffling the footfalls of all those who entered the busy lobby. It remained, faded and stained, burn marks off to one side from a forgotten small fire. An ancient chandelier hung in the center of the chilly room from a ceiling two stories high. On the wall, original oil paintings by an artist overlooked by history depicted California deserts by sunlight and by moonlight, cacti and sand and cruel rocky hills carefully colored an unreal lavender. The desk, to the left as you entered the lobby, retained a look of importance because of the fine wood of which it had been built. Although it had not recently been polished, over the years the oil from human hands had given it a warm

47

patina. A flight of wide carpeted stairs disappeared into the dim upper reaches. An old but functioning single elevator was located in the middle of the center wall.

Two people were in the lobby when Bennett entered: a young man with long, dark hair and a scraggly beard who sat behind the check-in desk, studying from books open before him, then making notes in a looseleaf binder; and, sitting on an ancient couch, a woman who might have been in her thirties or her sixties, her face so fully made-up it was difficult to tell. Her bright yellow hair was coiffed into curls and ringlets that covered her head like a shower cap. She wore nail polish and lipstick of a red so deep it looked black. Her wardrobe consisted of slim designer jeans, shoes with high spike heels, and a blouse of ruffles and lace under a fur coat that to Bennett's eye looked real and terribly expensive. He guessed it was probably mink, and wondered where she'd gotten it, and how long ago.

The young man at the desk glanced up from his books when Bennett entered. When he saw how disreputable Bennett looked he reached under the counter overhang for what Bennett knew would be a gun. Bennett gave the widest and most unhostile smile he could.

"Hey," he said, hands away from his body, fists open, everything about him nonthreatening. "How are you?"

The young man didn't say anything. He looked at Bennett warily, and his right hand remained under the counter.

"Sonny around?" Bennett asked.

The woman sitting on the couch looked up for the first time when Bennett said Sonny.

"Sonny?" the young man asked.

"He around?"

48

The young man's eyes darted toward the woman. Her face remained impassive, although it would have been difficult for her, with all the make-up, to have made any facial movement even if she'd wanted to.

"I told him I'd meet him here later," Bennett explained. "When I saw him a couple of hours ago I had another thing going on so I told him I'd meet him here later. He around? Have you seen him?"

The young man looked at the woman once again. Bennett thought he saw her shake her head, although the carefully arranged hair remained frozen in place.

"Hey," Bennett said, "I won't eat you. See? I'm harmless." He held his arms away from his body, to illustrate what a pussy-cat he was. "What you see is what you get," he said. "Just an acquaintance of Sonny's. Jesus, you act like I brought in the plague."

"He's not here," the young man said.

"He told me to meet him here," Bennett complained. "He told me he had a room here and I could meet him here and we'd have a drink. Shit. He was putting me on, is that what you're saying?"

Another look was exchanged between the young man and the woman on the couch.

"I'll be a son of a bitch," Bennett said. "Why in hell can't you give me a civil answer?" He turned and faced the woman. "You have any idea where Sonny is, lady?"

She seemed startled that he'd addressed her directly. "Sonny?" she asked in a husky voice. She either had a cold or years of booze had scarred her vocal chords.

"Yeah. You any idea where he is?"

She thought about it, then crossed her legs and let her foot swing idly, up and down, toe pointed as if aiming at something. "I know where he might be," she said at last.

"Where's that?" Bennett wanted to know.

"He might be anywhere but here," she said, attempting a smile. Her mouth only got halfway there, then didn't have the strength to continue and returned to its set position.

"Good," Bennett said dryly. "Very, very good. He might be anywhere but here," he mimicked. "Very nice." He turned so that he was addressing both of them. "That's what I call a warm and friendly reception," he complained. "Come in off the cold goddam street and the guy won't give you the time of day and the lady makes jokes when you ask a civil fucking question. Very nice," he repeated angrily. "Very fucking hospitable!"

As Bennett had hoped, the young man behind the desk hadn't been prepared for an outburst. He looked with something less than calm at the angry man in the center of the lobby, a man who needed a shave and a haircut and a bath, from the looks of him. A husky, muscular man with beady black eyes who suddenly made a fist of one hand and slammed it angrily into the palm of the other.

"Son of a bitch!" Bennett exclaimed.

"No reason to get uptight," the woman crooned. She patted the empty place on the couch beside her. "Sit down here and we'll have a nice talk while you wait for your friend. What was his name?"

"Sonny," Bennett said, accepting her offer and sitting beside her. He could smell hair spray, make-up, and stale perfume. This close he guessed she was closer to sixty than to thirty.

"Francis has to do his homework, and it makes him nervous when he's interrupted," she explained, gesturing toward the young man behind the desk. "Isn't that so, Francis?"

Francis nodded that it was so, and after a moment of indecision placed his right hand on the counter top, where Bennett could see it.

The woman turned back to Bennett. "Is Sonny a friend of yours?" she asked.

"Sort of," he said. "We know each other, Sonny and me. We got busted a couple of times together. We split a couple of handouts. We shared a bottle of wine. That kind of thing. Yeah. I guess you could say he's a friend of mine."

Outside on the empty street a bus went by, all the interior lights on, a single passenger sitting near the window in the center of the bus, the driver intent on finishing his run, each of them afraid of the other.

"I have friends like that," the woman said. "People I've shared a traumatic experience with." She let her hand rest for a moment on Bennett's knee. She wore so many large rings, the stones as big as boulders, that Bennett wondered if she'd ever be able to lift it. She did, simpering just a little, as if she'd found herself doing something she disapproved of, something that was completely out of character for her, but which she had done because of forces over which she had no control. "I don't believe I've seen you before," she said, having recovered her composure.

"Oh I've been around," Bennett said, squinting his eyes and glaring toward the door. "I've been around long enough to know when some little sonofabitch has been giving me shit."

"I'm sure," the woman said, "that if Sonny told you he'd be here, he'll be here. Sonny keeps his word."

So she knew him.

"Yeah, well . . ." Bennett grumbled. "Anybody got the time?"

The woman looked toward the young man behind

51

the desk. He stopped reading and with great effort referred to a wrist watch he wore on his right arm, pushed up halfway to the elbow, so anyone who wanted to steal something of value from him wouldn't be immediately aware of the watch. "Two-fifteen," he said, and went back to his books.

"Thank you, Francis," the woman said.

"Let me ask you something," Bennett said to the woman. "Sonny's a hell of a little guy. Right?"

"Oh yes," she agreed.

"I got this feeling from him when I first ran into him that he was something special. Don't you agree?"

"So are you," she said girlishly. "I had a feeling when you first walked in that door that you were something special. I had a feeling when you walked in that door that you were something else." She blinked her brown eyes. "In the vernacular," she said.

"Yeah?" Bennett asked. "Me, huh?"

"You," she said. She put her hand under his arm and squeezed. "Big strong you."

Francis looked up from his books. "Not in the lobby, for Chrissakes. Jesus!" He shook his head disgustedly and nervously tugged at his beard. Then, regaining his composure, he returned to his open book.

"You just mind your own business, Francis," the woman said. "Just mind your own bleeping business."

Francis began writing in his notebook, his pencil making jerky, angry movements. Bennett withdrew his arm from the woman's grasp and got to his feet.

"Hey?" he said to Francis. Angrily, the young man slapped down his pencil. "What kind of hours does Sonny keep? You're on all night, right?"

"I'm on all night," the young man said.

"What kind of hours does Sonny keep?" Bennett repeated. "I mean you sit there all night, you see him coming and going, what kind of hours does he keep?"

"Whatever hours he wants."

"For instance," Bennett said.

"He comes and goes, for Chrissakes," the young man said, a sharp edge developing in his voice. "He doesn't have to check the hell in and check the hell out, he comes and goes as he damn well pleases."

"He doesn't have to answer to anyone, that it?" Bennett said. "No wife, no girlfriend, no boyfriend?"

The woman on the couch snickered. "Oh that'll be the day," she said. "Sonny with a wife or a girlfriend or a boyfriend. That'll be the day. Right, Francis?"

"That'll be the day," Francis agreed.

"Well now," Bennett remarked, "you surprise me. What's this 'that'll be the day' talk? Something wrong with Sonny that I don't know about? Is that what you're trying to tell me?"

Francis and the woman exchanged a smirk.

"You want to tell him or should I?" Francis asked.

"Be my guest," the woman said, a silly smile on her face.

"You're full of shit and I'll tell you why," Francis began. "You're no friend of Sonny's because Sonny doesn't have any friends. Not one. Sonny doesn't say hello or good-bye to me or to her or to anyone alive. So when you come in here with all the bullshit about Sonny asked you to meet him here, her and me know you're full of the old bullshit because that's not the same Sonny we know." He turned his face toward the woman, who sat on the brocade-covered couch, her foot swinging faster than it had been. "Am I giving the straight story?" he asked her.

"Them's the facts, man," she said. "Oh, what bull-shit," she said, shaking her head sadly.

"So you see," Francis continued, "what the point to this conversation should be is not where's Sonny and what's he up to. The point to this conversation should be who the fuck are you and what're you up to, because you sure as hell aren't a friend of Sonny's because Sonny doesn't have any goddam friends and what you've been saying to us is pure and simple bullshit."

Bennett stood between them, smiling easily. "Well, goodness me," he said. "Here I thought I'd come into a place where nice people lived and worked and out of the blue I discover I'm with fucking vipers. Snakes!" he yelled, so suddenly they both jumped. "Distrustful people who are fucking paranoid!" he yelled. "Paranoid!" he repeated. "People who live in a little tiny goddam world where they're afraid to stick their ears out into the street and hear what the hell song the world is playing." He stopped and took a deep breath, and then looked up at the chandelier. "Do you believe this?" he asked the chandelier and the ceiling. "Do you really believe this? These two freaks are sitting here telling me about Sonny does this and Sonny does that and it's as clear as hell they don't know shit about Sonny. Not shit!" he yelled.

He'd succeeded in intimidating both of them. They looked nervously at one another. They'd begun to doubt themselves and what they'd thought was true about Sonny. They weren't sure any longer that what they would have sworn under oath was true about Sonny was really true.

"Let me ask you something," Bennett said to both of them. "You level with me now. No bullshitting. Level honest talk. I want you to be as honest with me as I'm being with you. Fair enough?"

They were numb. They nodded mutely.

"All right. Now here's the question. Why'd Sonny tell me to meet him here if he wasn't planning to come here? This is where he lives. Right?"

"Yeah. Right," Francis said.

"Right," Bennett said. "This is where he lives. Now why the hell would he tell me he'd meet me here if it wasn't so? You both know him, for Chrissakes, you've been giving me your goddam opinions about him, what sort of fella and so on, all free stuff a shrink wouldn't touch for a hundred and fifteen dollars. If Sonny told me he'd meet me here, why wouldn't he meet me? Anybody got any ideas?"

Francis nervously shrugged that he couldn't guess an answer to the question. Bennett faced the woman. She smiled politely, not wanting to upset the angry man standing in the center of the run-down lobby. "I can't imagine," she said. "I mean he told you he'd meet you here and then he doesn't show. I can't imagine why."

"Well," Bennett said in a reasonable tone of voice. "What could prevent a fella from keeping an appointment?"

"He got sick?" the woman suggested.

"That might be it," Bennett agreed. "What else?"

Francis leaped into the guessing game. "Well," he said, "he could have been in an accident."

"Right," Bennett said. "He could have been in an accident. What else?"

"Well," Francis continued, "he could have forgotten."

"He could have forgotten. Anything else might have slipped our minds?" He looked from one to the other.

"He wasn't ever planning to meet you?" the woman asked. She posed the question in a very small voice, fearful that once the words had been uttered Bennett would hop up and down and scream and perhaps do something dramatic or desperate.

But to her relief Bennett didn't get angry. "Now I think maybe we're getting closer to home," he said, nodding his head in vigorous agreement. "How do you read it?" he asked Francis.

Francis was chewing on the eraser of his pencil, nibbling at it as though it were a finely made chocolate dessert. "He was going to be busy later on and he didn't want you to know about it so he told you a lie."

Bennett expelled the air in his lungs as though he'd just surfaced after a deep-sea dive. "Bingo," he said. "I think you've hit the answer right on top of its head. Bingo," he repeated, softly and confidently. "Sonny had something else to do and so he told me this crap regarding time and place when he had no intention of keeping the appointment. His intention was to get the hell rid of me. What he doesn't know," he continued, smiling graciously at each of them, "is what a lucky thing happened. Because he told me that fucking horror story about time and place I had the opportunity to become acquainted with two nice, charming people who I probably might never have had the opportunity to meet under other conditions."

The woman purred like a pleased cat and Francis shit-kicked, his head down, doing everything but saying "Aw shucks, 'tweren't nothin'."

They heard the sirens at that moment. The woman and Francis were accustomed to that traumatic night noise and didn't change their position or their attitude. Bennett's ear, more finely tuned, identified a police car and, approaching from the opposite direction, an emergency ambulance.

"Well," he said to them, "it's been a real pleasure and an honor and I appreciate your hospitality. If

Sonny comes in looking for me explain that I hung around as long as I could and then nature called and I had to move along."

He sauntered to the door, being careful not to run, not to race to where the sirens were heading.

"Perhaps our paths will cross another day," he said from the door. "Until then . . ." he blew a kiss toward the woman, snapped a starchy half-salute at Francis, and ducked out into the street. The approaching police car passed him, lights and siren working, motor roaring, speeding toward the blocks where the others were. Bennett broke into a trot and followed. A man facing an alley wall turned at the noise and Bennett could see fresh urine shining in the street light.

White wasn't on his block, nor was Sean MacManus on his. Ahead, three blocks from where Bennett would have been working had he stayed on the street, the police car had stopped beside an emergency ambulance parked alongside the curb, flashing lights reflecting in a store window on which "Last Sale We Quit" had been painted in thick white letters. He saw the attendants working over a disheveled man who lay crumpled in the street. Standing around this group he recognized Tom White and Sean MacManus, who turned when they heard him approaching.

"Charlie?" Bennett asked.

"Yeah," Sean replied. "He'll be all right. I saw this little weasel jump him and got here as fast as I could, but the bastard was gone before I got here. Tommy was right behind me."

"He's a real sprinter," Tom White said. "Zipped out like a jackrabbit." He made zigzag motions with his hand.

Bennett leaned over Charlie Simpson, who lay on

the pavement, a folded blanket under his head. The paramedics were bandaging his right leg.

"How you doing?" Bennett asked, crouching down beside the paramedic.

"Bennett," Charlie greeted him. "Pretty good. You're right. He's a quick little sonofabitch."

Bennett looked inquiringly at the paramedic, a young man with a moon face and neatly cropped blond hair. "No severe damage," he said. "No arteries or muscles or tendons severed. Just a deep cut. They'll sew it up at the hospital."

When he finished the temporary bandage, he and his partner picked up Charlie and laid him on the gurney, covered him with a sheet, extended the gurney, and wheeled it to the rear of the emergency ambulance. Bennett walked alongside.

"Did you get a look at him?" Bennett asked Charlie Simpson.

"Exactly what you described," Charlie said, his sad face pale. "Small, quick, strong as hell, dressed all in black, quiet as a mouse. So he must wear rubber soles, thick ones—that crepe material, probably."

"Was he wearing a mask?" Bennett asked.

"Oh, yeah. That weird-looking porcelain gadget you described," Charlie said. "That's enough to startle a person, I can tell you. You sort of sense he's there behind you and you turn to see this goddam mask. Wildest thing you ever saw," he told the paramedics. "You don't know what in hell you're looking at. It's like you were in front of a store window where they were displaying cosmetics or beauty things of that type, and they had decorated the window with these porcelain faces and as you looked one of them moved and was attached to a body that had a knife in its hand ready to slash you." He reached down to his leg. "Which he did. Shit, if I hadn't rolled away he'd have shoved it into my gut or opened my neck."

"Tommy?" Bennett called, as the attendants lifted the gurney into the ambulance.

White jogged over to them.

"Ride to the hospital with him," Bennett said. Charlie started to protest. "You just shut up," Bennett said. "You might remember something that's important to us and you can tell Tommy."

The paramedics hopped out and Tommy got in and sat beside Charlie.

"You okay, buddy?" he asked.

"Oh, Christ, I'm too old and dried out to get hurt. Did you ever try to kill a prune?" Charlie asked as the attendants closed and fastened the rear doors. Bennett stood back as they slid into the front seat, started up the ambulance with a quiet roar, hit the siren, and pulled out.

The two cops who'd been in the squad car were talking to Sean. By the time Bennett reached them they were preparing to leave.

"You guys have all the fun," one of them said dryly. "Lying around on the pavement waiting for somebody to kill you."

"Lucky bastards," said the other, getting into the black-and-white.

They turned off their flashers and quietly drove away. "What the hell happened?" Bennett asked Sean. "Did you see any of it?"

"No," Sean said. "Tommy yelled. He was checking me, and me him, and he saw past me to Charlie. I don't know where the little bastard came from. I'd checked Charlie just a second before and he was all right, kind of hunkered in this doorway." He showed Bennett a recessed doorway, the entrance to a

59

boarded-up building. "I waved to check him, he returned the wave. I turned around to check Tommy and the shit hit the fan. Tommy yelled and pointed. The guy was taking off that way, zigging and zagging like it was a goddam war zone." He shook his head in wonder. "Christ, if Tommy hadn't yelled, or if Charlie hadn't rolled when he did . . . I mean, that little sonofabitch with the knife is one fast mother."

They went back over the ground together, examining the place where the attack had occurred, and then following the assailant's path as he'd raced away. The area was clean of clues.

"I don't think he'll be back," Bennett said, "but we'll stick around for another hour or so. Then we can knock off."

They stayed on the cold street until first light. Tommy White rejoined them when Charlie was safely in the hospital. Bennett arranged the next night's meeting and, exhausted, the men went home.

5

Polly was in the kitchen, sitting at the breakfast table, a cup of coffee before her, wearing a robe over her nightgown, when Bennett walked into the house. She looked as though she'd been crying. He went to her and kissed the top of her head. She didn't look up at him and might not have known he was there.

"Hon," he said.

She didn't respond.

"Hey," he said. "You all right?"

He sat in the chair opposite her. When she looked up he saw the tears in her eyes.

"What happened?" he asked.

"I had the radio on," she said. "I heard the news. I thought it was you."

He reached across the table and took her hand. "Now you know nothing's going to happen to me," he said.

She shook her head. "That's just not enough," she said. "It's just not enough for you to tell me that. It could happen to you just as easily as it happened to . . . who was it? The news report didn't identify him as a police officer."

"Charlie Simpson."

"So it could just as easily have been you. Isn't that right?"

"If you mean Charlie was unlucky and some night I might be unlucky, yes, I suppose you could say it might have happened to me. . . ."

"It did the other night," she interrupted, her voice shrill. "He tried to kill you the other night. Why do you keep saying lucky and unlucky? What's that got to do with it? If you weren't there on the street we wouldn't be talking about bad luck and good luck. There'd be no need for it, because you wouldn't be in a position where a crazy man with a knife could kill you!"

He squeezed her hand. "Now hon," he said. "You're upset because that damn news report scared you a little. . . ."

"A *little*?" She pulled her hand free and turned away from him, staring out the kitchen window, looking into the neat back garden she was so proud of. The early morning sun lighted camellia bushes heavy with red blossoms and two enormous birds of paradise, whose unreal flowers seemed about to fly away. "I wasn't scared a little," she said. "I was terrified. The news report said a man had been hurt, slashed, police felt sure it had been done by the same person who'd committed the murders, and I just knew you were the one who'd been hurt."

"Let's have some coffee," he said, getting himself a cup and saucer from the cabinet. She'd made a full pot, and he lifted it from the stove and refreshed her cup, then poured for himself.

"I don't know what to do," she said when he was seated. "I know you love what you're doing, and I don't know how to handle my part of it."

"When this is out of the way I'll see if I can't get

something that's a little less dangerous," he suggested, not really meaning what he said. He still felt that her fear, her strong feelings about what he did, would somehow dissolve or dry up or magically disappear.

"You don't mean that, and you won't do it." She brushed back her hair and held it, long blonde hair pulled away from her face by a slender hand, unpolished nails perfectly shaped. "I sound like one of the hags in a million plays, always complaining, always nagging. I'm not only bored listening to myself, I'm getting so I don't particularly like me." She looked right at him, deep blue eyes fastened like magnets on him. "You know how much I love you," she said softly.

"Yeah. I know."

"And I know how much you love me. That's not the subject. You understand that."

He nodded that he understood. He wasn't sure if he could form words, if his voice would work, if speech would clearly come, unencumbered by the sadness he felt for both of them. He was doing the only thing he enjoyed doing and knew how to do and had been trained to do, and it was beginning to destroy her.

He finally got some words out. "It's a mess," is what he said.

"Yes it is."

"But I don't think we should talk about it now."

"Because you're tired and you just finished work," she finished it for him.

"I guess I say that most of the time."

"Most of the time," she nodded. "But that's all right. At least you're not malicious about it. I have a tendency to feel so sorry for myself that I get very bitchy now and then."

63

He started to say no you don't, but instead, grinned, and said: "You can say that again."

She laughed. "If you weren't so tired I'd wallop you for that remark. I'd knock you from here clear across the room. That's what I'd do to you if you weren't so tired."

He drank some of his coffee as she watched him, loving him with her eyes. "Fred?" And when he looked up, "I'm sorry. I was scared. Really scared. It's awful, waiting. The other day I got real mad at myself. Suppose he'd gone off to fight in a Crusade? I said to myself. Suppose it was another time, and he'd gone away to make a home for us in a faraway place? What would you do then? I asked myself."

"Except it's not another time. It's now. It's something we have to deal with now," he said quietly. "You're absolutely right, and you shouldn't tell yourself otherwise, or try to con yourself that it isn't so by comparing now to another time. What I do is tough on me and twice as tough on you because you have to sit here and wait for me to come home with the story of what happened. I'm there. I don't have to wait. I know what happened."

"You'd better get some sleep," she said, standing and taking her cup to the sink.

He followed her and kissed the back of her neck. "We're going to make it all right, hon," he told her. "You'll see."

But he didn't really believe it. He appreciated and understood her concern for him, her fear for what might happen to him in his job. But he wasn't able to face the fact that things would be better between them only when he was out of police work and doing something safer. He fell asleep trying to figure ways of making her content, as she had been when they had first

Bennett slammed his fist into his thigh. "Shit!" he said. He angrily surveyed the ceiling. "He's known as Sonny. He has a room at the Majestic. Now go out and fuck it up."

"Description?"

"Five-four or -five. Can't tell the age. I've never seen his face, he wears this porcelain mask. He weighs probably one-twenty to one-forty, slight, wiry, strong little sonofabitch, can't give you color of hair or eyes because he's always covered up. Dressed in black, shoes with rubber or crepe soles, black slacks, black sweater up around his neck, probably a turtleneck, black watch-cap."

"You're sure he lives at the Majestic?" Drang asked.

"No, I'm not sure. I haven't seen him check in or out. I wouldn't know him if I saw him, as I've explained." Bennett leaned back in his chair and wiggled his bare toes. "I'm not even sure his name is Sonny. I've been told a man named Sonny hangs out in that neighborhood, dresses as our suspect dresses, fits the same generally loose physical description. That's what I've been told. I haven't succeeded in putting it all together, which is why I hadn't given you the information. It's a little early in the investigation to be arresting people because of how they dress." He scratched one foot against another, comfortably, like a waking cat. "Who told you I had this information?"

"Sean MacManus," Drang said, then added quickly, "He wasn't telling tales. He thought you'd already passed it on to me. Asked me what I thought about it. Seemed to be pleased as hell with what you'd come up with. Gave you all the credit. He thinks you're one of the smartest cops on the force."

"Well, you can't fault him on that," was Bennett's modest comment. "There aren't many of us who let a really supercrazy person slide right out from between their fingers two nights running. That's not easy to do. That, Captain, takes brains, which Sean appears to have recognized."

Whenever Drang was about to say something portentous, he had the habit of placing his index fingers together in front of his mouth and frowning, as if at the same time he was about to speak and stay quiet. He did this now until he had Bennett's complete attention.

"Whether or not you agree," he said to Bennett, "I want you to stay on detached duty, but not on the street. I want you to find out who this Sonny is and whether or not he has anything to do with those murders."

"Decisions on procedure are my own?" Bennett asked.

Drang swung his hand this way and that. "Up to a point," he said. "We can't have a member of the force giving the department a bad name. If you go too far we'll disown you."

"Who's my contact?"

"Me," Drang said. "For your cover I'm officially giving you a leave of absence to recover from physical ailments caused by this person we're trying to apprehend."

"Physical ailments?" Bennett's eyebrows pointed at the hairline.

"Two nights ago, when the murderer attacked you, you were hurt. Although you didn't report it, I found out and you're officially on a leave of absence recovering."

"I need money. For personal expenses and paying snitches. I have a hunch there'll be a lot of those. Cash, no checks."

"I'll take care of it," Drang assured him. "About the same as what you've been spending on other deals like this one?"

Something in his tone made Bennett hesitate before immediately answering. "What's that mean?" he asked.

"What?"

"You sounded like someone doesn't like me paying snitches for information. True or false?" Bennett's eyes were fixed on Drang. He'd learned to read him, over the years, and it was important, before he agreed to take this assignment, to know if there was going to be any hassle about expenses. Because Bennett was in the habit of drawing reasonably large cash sums from the department to make payoffs for information otherwise unavailable, some by-the-rule-book officials had thought they were onto a case of under-the-table corruption when they first heard about it. There'd been talk of putting a stop to the payments, but once it was proved to be a common police procedure the matter had been dropped. Now, however, it seemed to Bennett it was being brought up again. "Well?" he repeated. "Is that true or false?"

Drang hemmed and hawed. "I'm being overly cautious," he said at last. "It's not that anything's come up recently, it's more that I don't want anything to come up."

Bennett looked as if he didn't believe him.

"God's truth," Drang said.

"Um-hmm," was Bennett's noncommittal comment.

"Anyway," Drang continued, "I'm sure you'll be careful with the money." Bennett looked up angrily. "As you always are," Drang said, trying to make peace. "I'm not the one who complained about spending. I'm the one who's in favor of it. It's something that must be done."

"Bet your ass," Bennett growled.

They sat quietly for a few minutes, each man thinking his own thoughts, planning his own moves, writing his own scenario of what the next days would be like. Bennett finished his coffee in a gulp. "That it?" he asked.

"Yeah, I guess so," Drang replied. He started for the kitchen with his empty coffee cup.

"Leave it on the tray," Bennett said. "I'll take it in. Polly?" he called.

She came back into the room. "Finished?" she asked.

"Thanks for the coffee," Drang said. "See you." He kissed her cheek. "Stay in touch," he told Bennett, and then left the house.

Polly picked up the tray and carried it into the kitchen, Bennett padding along beside her, his bare feet slapping the lineoleum floor.

"What were you talking about?" she asked, setting the tray on the tile counter and rinsing the cups and saucers.

"I'm not on the street any more," Bennett told her.

Surprised, she turned to face him. "What? I don't understand."

"I'm on detached service, checking out a suspect," he said proudly, as if he'd just accomplished an extraordinary feat. "How about them apples?"

She was confused. "I still don't understand what . . . ?"

"I'm off the street," he said. "My own hours, I'm in charge, I decide what to do and how to do it in the matter of checking out a very important suspect."

"But . . . well, that's . . ." she grinned happily. He put his arms around her and kissed her.

"Relieved?" he asked her.

She nodded. "I think so. I'm still not sure what . . ."

He kissed her again and didn't let her finish. Then, excited, he said: "It's what I've been working toward, hon. It's exactly the way I want to operate. I'm a member of the department, I love that, but I escape the bullshit, you know? I'm trusted enough to be allowed to go out and work on a case the way I think it should be done. It's great. It's really great. And you don't have to worry," he told her. "I'm not going to be lying on a pavement downtown, making believe I'm an old drunk, begging for a crazy to come kill me. You feel better now?" he asked her.

He's like a boy, she thought as she looked at him, at his honest delight with what had just happened. "I think it's great," she said. "It's about time," she added.

When he hugged her again she could feel his arousal.

"Come on inside," he said, and led her back into the darkened bedroom.

They made love, and it was better than it had been for more than a year.

6

By night darkness covered many of the wrinkles and blemishes in the lobby of the Majestic hotel. By day sagging chairs, which in shadow had appeared to be in fairly good condition, were revealed as decrepit, standing on their last legs. The aging carpet now exposed bare patches where it was balding. The ancient chandelier, hanging from a ceiling two stories above the lobby floor, was rusted and missing many crystals that, long ago, had glittered in soft light. Even the sound of the elevator was different, noisier than it should have been, each trip a defiance of all nature's laws, motion accompanied by groaning and squealing, starts and stops accompanied by a shuddering movement, like an old person with a sudden feverish chill.

Neither Francis, the young night clerk, nor the woman in the fur coat was there when Bennett walked in. He hadn't shaved, but he had combed his hair and put on clean jeans and a windbreaker, and the impression he gave was that here was a man trying to grow a beard, a man who worked out of doors, a tough hard man, eyes like black onyx. Several people loitered in the lobby, sitting on the faded furniture reading newspapers or magazines as old as they were, some of them just staring at the badly painted oils that hung on the walls. Replacing Francis behind the desk was a ferret-faced man of about forty whose eyes darted about the room suspiciously. He was dressed in a shiny blue suit, a white shirt becoming threadbare at the collar, a striped tie, and an old hand-knit woolen scarf, which he wore loosely around his shoulders although it was not cold in the lobby. His roving eyes caught Bennett and locked there. He recognized a stranger. What he had to determine was whether the stranger was friend or foe. In his world, foe first came to mind.

Bennett walked to the desk. The clerk waited for him to speak. "How much are your rooms?" Bennett asked.

"Twelve-fifty a day and up," the clerk said. His voice was surprisingly strong, with an edge that cut through all other sounds. He could have worked as foreman in a boiler factory and given clearly heard orders without shouting.

"Up to where?" Bennett inquired.

"There's a suite on the top floor," the clerk replied.

"How much is it?" Bennett wanted to know.

"The suite has a living room, one bedroom, kitchenette, and bath with a sunken tub and a stall shower. It goes for sixty bucks a day." He studied Bennett more carefully. "One week in advance," he added.

"You're concerned because I don't have luggage," Bennett guessed. "Well that's because I'm not prepared to move in this second. I'm making inquiries. After I've shopped around I'll make a decision."

"Nicely thought out. Of course," the clerk responded. His eyes were small and very close together and he squinted at any suggestion of bright light. Bennett guessed that if the clerk were to smile he'd show small, sharp teeth like a rodent's.

"I'd like to see the suite before I make up my mind," Bennett said.

"I can't show it to you right this moment," the clerk said. "I'm attached to the desk until eleven."

"That's all right, I'll look at it," Bennett said, holding out his hand. "Give me the key and I'll look it over and then return the key when I come back downstairs."

Astonished at Bennett's gall, the clerk stared at him.

"Listen," Bennett lied, "I'm going to level with you. This is not for me. A guy gave me ten bucks to look for a room for him in here. Now come on, I've got to have an answer for him. I can't go back on the street and say to him, I don't know what the suite on the top floor looks like, I didn't get to see it. He'd be pissed off at me if I did that. For an example, suppose it was you out there who gave me ten and told me to find a place for you to stay . . ."

"Why don't he come in and look for himself?" the clerk asked.

"Now that's a good question," Bennett said. "A damn good question. The same thought occurred to me. But I have to tell you I haven't got an answer for you. I haven't the faintest damn idea why this guy didn't do this himself."

As they talked the clerk's weasel eyes had been flicking to either side of Bennett's head, scouting the lobby, checking entrances and exits. Now they locked on a spot to Bennett's right, and behind him. A place just below Bennett's shoulder.

"Want me to show him the suite, Maurice?" someone behind Bennett asked.

The clerk seemed doubtful. He didn't immediately

say yes please, the way he would have if he desperately wanted to get Bennett off his back. He thought about the request. Bennett wanted to turn around but didn't.

"What the hell," the voice said, "maybe he's telling the truth. If he's full of it no harm done, he sees it and goes. If he's telling the truth you just got yourself a guest who's staying in the suite."

It was a persuasive argument. "That's true," the clerk had to agree.

"Sure it is," the voice said.

The clerk made up his mind. He turned and slid a key from one of the pigeon holes built into the wall behind him, then turned back and held it out.

"Here you go," he said.

"Thanks," the voice said.

"Sonny'll show you the room," the clerk said to Bennett.

The man who'd been identified as Sonny stood beside Bennett, the key in his right hand. He was slight, no more than five-feet-three or -four inches tall. He was wiry, as a gymnast would be, with a delicate, feminine face, full-lipped, with large reddish-brown eyes and a delicate nose with a light scar crossing the bridge. He was dressed in a polo shirt and faded green gabardine slacks, and he wore tennis shoes. Everything about him was immaculate. Bennett thought, in that first glance, that he looked like a replica of the Ken doll that partners Barbie.

"This way," Sonny said, walking toward the elevator. Bennett followed. Sonny opened accordion gates and held them while Bennett entered the ancient cage. Sonny followed, letting the gates slam shut. He pressed a button marked *P*, and with a protesting groan the elevator shuddered, then began to rise slowly.

"I certainly appreciate this," Bennett told Sonny.

"No sweat," Sonny replied. He stood erect and trim in the center of the elevator, watching the wall descend in front of him. As they passed each floor, Bennett could read a fading number. The elevator jerked to a stop at the letter *P*. Sonny folded back the accordion elevator door, and then manipulated the floor door open. Bennett stepped out, Sonny behind him.

"The penthouse Maurice told you is free is at the end of this hall," Sonny said, leading the way. The hall was wide, lit by protruding sconces shaped to resemble tree limbs. The carpet was in better condition than the one that covered the lobby floor, evidence that this hallway hadn't borne the traffic the lobby had. They passed several shut doors as they walked.

"Other rooms up here?" Bennett asked.

"Not any more," Sonny said. "Maurice told me once upon a time this was the owner's apartment, this whole floor, when the place was first built, back in the nineteen twenties. Now it's just the penthouse on this floor, these other rooms are offices, or bedrooms for special friends." He stopped and looked at Bennett, his strange eyes alight. "You can imagine," he said softly.

"Oh, yeah," Bennett agreed, wondering if the vice squad knew about these top-floor rooms.

Sonny continued staring at Bennett. He'd cocked his head, as if he were measuring him. "Do I know you?" he asked, after an uncomfortable silence.

"Maybe," Bennett said. "I've been around. Here and there. You might have seen me, sure."

Sonny continued to stare. "I'm sure I know you," he said.

"I wouldn't doubt it," Bennett said. "Name's Bennett."

"Not by your name," Sonny said.

Somehow Bennett was standing with his back to the

wall at the end of the dead end hall. The only light, aside from that thrown by the sconces, came from the opposite end of the hall, where a red exit sign identified an emergency door, the top half of which was reinforced glass through which sunlight streamed, leaving Sonny's face in half-shadow, and Bennett's harshly lighted. The two men eyed each other. Sonny moved first, starting toward Bennett, who felt his muscles tighten with apprehension.

"Excuse me," Sonny said as he stepped past Bennett and opened the door at the end of the hall. "This is it," he said.

Bennett entered a room out of another time. It was a place Fitzgerald might have described or John Held drawn. The large living room was bone white and furnished with white sofas and chairs. Tables and other wood surfaces were painted white, and milk white table lamps were strategically placed. The carpet was a thick white shag. The single bedroom could be seen on the right, and the kitchenette adjoined a small bar on the left. Both areas had also been painted white.

"Nice," Bennett said. "Very nice."

Sonny walked into the bedroom and Bennett followed. The ceiling was mirrored above an enormous round bed covered with a thick white quilt. Beyond, Bennett could see the sunken tub in the bathroom.

"As advertised," he said to Sonny.

Sonny nodded, and walked to the kitchenette. When Bennett got there, the little man had opened all the drawers to show cutlery, dishes, and the utensils with which a sandwich or breakfast, but not a large meal, could be prepared.

Sonny lifted a steak knife from a drawer and balanced it on his index finger. "I guess you could fry a steak in here," he said.

77

"I don't know why not," Bennett agreed.

"What's he looking for?" Sonny asked. "This man hired you?"

"Hard to tell," Bennett said. "He didn't give me a clue."

"Because he doesn't exist?" Red-brown eyes flamed suspiciously. Sonny moved his hand so that the steak knife swayed up and down, perfectly balanced, the thin sharp blade catching light as it moved.

Bennett shifted gears. "How'd you figure that out?" he asked admiringly.

Sonny hadn't expected the quick admission. "I just figured it," he said.

"You're right, there's no guy." Bennett leaned forward conspiratorially and lowered his voice. "I wanted a chance to look around in here. I thought what's his name, Maurice? that he'd give me the key and I could take my time and case the joint. I never figured a smart guy like you would come along. You're sharp," he admitted.

Sonny was unprepared for the reply. His hand stopped moving and once again the knife was still, perfectly balanced. "Why case the joint?" he asked.

Bennett's face was disbelieving. "Come on," he said.

"There's nothing in this building," Sonny said.

"There's always a little something you can turn into a buck or two," Bennett said. "You know that."

"Like what?"

"Money, jewelry, you know."

"They don't have a well-to-do clientele."

"People have to eat, right? People didn't spring full-blown into the world, they were begat, like it says. Which means mommas and daddies. Which means the family jewels, watches, broaches, you know. For example I got a watch my old daddy left me when he passed on, a railroad watch, you know the kind? You carry it in your pocket in your vest and you take it out and open the case to see what time it is." As he spoke Bennett demonstrated in pantomime how he would take out of his vest pocket a nonexistent watch, given to him by a father who wasn't a railroad man, and read the time. "It's so valuable I don't carry it with me," Bennett said. "Anybody who knows the time of day, he'd see that watch and whap! that's it, I've had it and he's off and running. That's the sort of item anyone's liable to be carrying or more likely has left in his or her room, whichever the case may be."

Sonny heard him out, eyes glittering. "There was a guy here last night looking for me," he said.

"That so?"

"Right. This guy had a song and a dance about how he and me had an appointment, which was at my suggestion that he meet me here, which this guy was doing. Although that was a lie. There was no appointment. Why would you tell a lie? Hmm?"

Bennett shifted his weight. "Why would you think it was me?" Bennett asked.

"It was you." Sonny was definite. "It was you surer than hell. I mean, if it wasn't you who the hell else was it? I mean how many people come barging into this old fleabag with these tall stories about appointments and about checking things out because of all the valuables lying around for the taking. I mean, the only person who'd do that would be a wacko." He looked up at Bennett. He was standing on the balls of his feet, as if he were going to leap into the air at any moment. "You. Correct?"

"As a matter of fact, you're exactly correct," Bennett easily confessed. "Me to a T," he said. "But I don't think I ever considered myself a wacko. Down on my luck, yeah. Struggling to make ends meet, you betcha. A man who'll use any excuse to get what he wants, you can count on it. But wacko? I don't think so."

"Then why'd you make up that bull about you and me?"

"I already told you that," Bennett said. "I explained to you how I wanted to case this joint. I didn't figure the lady was going to be here last night. . . ."

"Lady!" Sonny sniggered.

"Well, whatever," Bennett said. "What I figured was it was late, you know? and there wouldn't be anyone here but the night clerk kid, what's his name . . ."

"Francis."

"Francis, right, and I figured I'd wander around, he wouldn't pay any attention when I said I was waiting for you, and sonofabitch that lady was here and started chattering to me about this and that and I never got to do what I began to do, which was case the joint, and so that's why I'm here today."

Bennett wasn't able to tell if Sonny was accepting all of this nonsense. Red-brown eyes stared gravely, without a hint of what was going on behind them.

"How'd you know I lived here?" Sonny asked. "I mean, you come walking in here with your story about you and me meeting. Where'd my name come into it? Why me?"

Good question, Bennett thought. *Damn good question.*

Sonny waited for an answer.

"I didn't know you lived here," Bennett said at last. "I was going to stall until I found something that would let me hang around." So far so good, he thought. Sonny accepted that. "Then, two seconds after I walked into the lobby, I heard the lady say something about Sonny. Whatever it was, it gave me the idea somebody named Sonny lived here, so that's how you got mixed up in this."

They stood silently while Sonny considered what had been said, and whether or not he wanted to do anything about it. Then, instead of responding, Sonny said: "If you're finished up here, I got things to do." He carefully placed the knife back in the drawer.

"Yeah. Well, I'm finished," Bennett said.

The short, athletic man had turned away and was standing in the hallway waiting. As soon as Bennett left the penthouse apartment, Sonny closed and double-locked the door, then led the way to the elevator.

They rode down without speaking. Maurice was on the phone with someone when they reached the lobby. Sonny walked to the hotel door and opened it for Bennett.

"Thanks for your time," Bennett said.

"You ought to watch yourself," Sonny said. "You could get in trouble if you don't watch yourself."

"Appreciate the advice," Bennett told him as he stepped out onto the sidewalk.

He stood there, watching to see if Sonny spoke to Maurice. The little man walked back to the desk and dropped the key. Maurice glanced up from his phone conversation, but Sonny had already gone back to the elevator. He opened the accordion gates and stepped in. The gates closed behind him and the elevator rose out of view.

Sonny hadn't told the desk clerk anything about Bennett and their conversation. Score one.

7

The man was seated beside a bank of public telephones in the waiting room of the downtown intercity bus terminal. He had a pencil in his hand and the Racing Form in his lap and he was marking his selections at every track the paper listed. Occasionally he would refer to his wristwatch and then, as confirmation, he'd crook his neck around and stare up at the clock that hung on the wall above the departure gates. He was a heavyset man with a jolly face and pleasant blue eyes that seemed to be always smiling. He was casually dressed in well-pressed slacks and a tweed jacket with suede patches at the elbows and shoulders, protection from the wear and tear caused by hunting rifles and country pubs, with neither of which he had any familiarty. By profession he was a snitch—he made it his business to know what was going on, and he knew who he could relay that information to and how much it was worth. His hobby was handicapping horses. His name was Roger Beauchamp, and for a reason no one ever understood, he was called Pinky. Bennett went directly to him and sat down on the bench beside him. Pinky didn't move his head, but his pleasant blue eyes quickly shifted to see who was there.

"Bennett?" he said, not able to suppress his surprise. "What the hell are you doing? What kind of a way is that for an officer of the law to be seen in public?" He put down his Racing Form and pencil. "I thought you guys had a dress code—and rules about beards and moustaches? If you're here to get my opinion and advice, I say you haven't the face for a beard or a moustache, it makes you look like the villain in a cheap spaghetti western." He stopped long enough to take a deep breath. "How the hell are you?" he asked. "Long time no see."

"How's it going?" Bennett asked.

"Well you know, you win some, you lose some," Pinky said. "Somewhat the pattern of life. Here today, gone tomorrow." His friendly face smiled at Bennett. "It's really very nice to see you, even if you look like shit," he said. "Is that your uniform when you're undercover, or have you been fired from the force and you're practically destitute and on the streets?"

"I have something I want you to do," Bennett said. He fished a bill from his pocket. "It's worth twenty to get you started. Fifty if you come up with what I want."

"Fifty additional?"

"Total of fifty."

Pinky thought about it. "Now you understand if you want someone killed, that's more than fifty. I can't clear bad guys off the streets for fifty."

"I don't want anyone killed. Now or ever before. When in hell have I ever asked for someone to be killed?" Bennett wanted to know.

"Now now now," Pinky said, "I was just testing to get some idea of what it is you want me to do. I'm a man with certain standards by which I live and I want that out on the table right from the start."

"Okay, it's out on the table. What I need is some information. Then, later on, if you get me what I want, there might be some future business."

"Well, information doesn't come cheap," Pinky said, leaning back on the bench. "Information has value. If I could tell you how long someone was going to live, or what the stock market was going to do, or which of these gee-gees was sure to win, that information would be very valuable and would cost a great deal of money."

"It's not that kind of information."

The loudspeaker cracked on and an accented voice announced that the bus for San Diego, with stops en route, was about to load, and passengers should proceed to gate four. This announcement was repeated in Spanish. A young man in a marine uniform picked up his duffel and walked to the departure gate. He was joined there by an old man in overalls who was chewing tobacco, and a neatly dressed, slender woman with white hair who appeared to have been crying.

"Explain," Pinky said.

Bennett lowered his voice, and Pinky leaned forward. "A man named Sonny lives at the Majestic," Bennett explained. "I want information about him."

Pinky nodded. "Can do," he said. "What sort of information? Girls? Boys?"

"Everything you can find out," Bennett said. "His full name, where he's from, how long he's been living at the Majestic."

"I'll check around," Pinky agreed. "I'm familiar with people who frequent that particular establishment. It shouldn't be too difficult to get one or two answers." He leaned back on the bench and stared at the travelers now entering the gate leading to the bus that would soon leave for San Diego and points en route.

84

"Did you see the old lady who was crying?" he asked Bennett.

"Yeah."

"Why, I wonder?" Pinky asked. "I sit here and I watch life as it passes by and I wonder why's this person doing that, why's that person doing something else. And I see an old lady like that about to board a bus for San Diego and she's been crying and I wonder why."

"She just said goodbye to her daughter and her grandchild," Bennett said, gesturing toward the street entrance to the terminal where a young woman stood, holding a small child in her arms. She waved toward the boarding gate, and the elderly woman waved back and smiled.

"I didn't notice them," Pinky said somewhat sheepishly. "I was looking the other way."

"You gotta watch that," Bennett said. "Looking the other way can get you killed." He stood. "I'll meet you here about four this afternoon. See what you can find out."

"I'll get right on it," Pinky said.

Bennett left him sitting there and reached the street entrance in time to hold the door open for the young woman with the child. She thanked him and hurried away, sniffling. Bennett headed in the opposite direction.

He walked the four or five blocks toward the shopping center of the city, where great department stores occupied granite block buildings that looked like archaeological relics beside the shining new steel and reflecting-glass skyscrapers that surrounded and dwarfed them. He was more interested in displays than merchandise, and studied windows where male and female mannequins suggestively posed in bedrooms, or sat, about to picnic, beneath false trees, or stood uncomfortably still in warm garments before backdrops of icy blue. In one window, kitchenware was stacked in precarious pyramids, and tables in a variety of sizes had been placed on edge so that their wood-block tops could be seen. In other stores there were displays of cosmetics and displays of resort wear, and only when Bennett reached a window that was being decorated with a great stuffed turkey, arranged among branches of autumn leaves foreign to the city, did he realize that it was fall and the Thanksgiving holiday was close by. A young man was decorating the window in which the turkey played a prominent part, and Bennett entered the store and stood beside the opening through which the display artist carried the objects to be placed on view. When the young man reached out for a leafy branch, Bennett pleasantly said, "That's going to be a beautiful window display."

The young man smiled but didn't reply. He was the thinnest man Bennett had ever seen, probably in his late twenties, with scraggly blond hair and a pale, worried face. He wore jeans without a label in back, and a pale yellow shirt with the sleeves rolled up to expose scrawny arms. He disappeared back into the window with the leafy branch, and Bennett watched him carefully place it above the stuffed turkey.

When he appeared again, Bennett said, "Hard to believe it's nearly Thanksgiving."

"Which means Christmas is on the way. That's when we get busy," the young man said, stressing the word "that's" so heavily the rest of the sentence was nearly inaudible. "But it's fun," he admitted. He wiped his hands on a cloth that hung from his belt like the towel a quarterback uses to keep his hands dry, then carefully picked up a fake rock and carried it out into the display window. Bennett had the feeling he was standing backstage at a theater, that these were story props for a show he would never see. After a moment the young man came back and saw that Bennett was still standing there.

"Did you want something?" he asked.

"I wanted to ask you a question," Bennett said. "A couple of months ago, I think it was, I'm not good at dates, you had a window, I think it was this store, and there were these beautiful masks in the display. I think they were of porcelain, arched eyebrows, little tiny turned up nose, carefully made-up lips . . ."

"Oh yes. Everyone's using them now. I think we were the first," the young man said. "You liked the display?"

"Oh, I thought it was just great," Bennett said enthusiastically. "Really great."

"Thank you," the young man said, making a sort of half-bow, half-curtsy.

"Where'd you get them?" Bennett asked.

"Montcrieff's," the young man said. "The masks are lovely."

"Montcrieff's," Bennett repeated.

"They're on the west side," the young man said. "Did you want to buy one?"

"Well, let me tell you what I was thinking, and you tell me if it's a good idea." He touched his unshaven face. "I'm trying to grow a beard for this costume party my wife's planning to give at Thanksgiving." The young man was relieved to have Bennett's unshaven face explained. "I'd described these masks to my wife and she thought she'd wear one of them, and we'd kind of look different from anyone else there, me with a beard and she in this mask." Bennett stopped talking because the young man was smiling and shaking his head.

"That's not possible," the young man said. "Those masks aren't made for wearing. They're flat-surfaced in back. Your wife couldn't put it on. You can't wear them." The thin hands illustrated how the mask would sit on the front of the face, but not curve around the sides. "It wouldn't stay on, do you see what I mean?" he asked.

"I think so, yeah," Bennett answered. "She'll really be disappointed," he said. "She was counting on wearing one of those masks." He thought about it, his face sad. "I wonder if these people, Montcrieff's, could make a mask like that that could be worn?"

"I would think they could," the young man said. "They do a great deal of work for the motion-picture industry. They're in the book."

"I really appreciate this," Bennett said.

"Oh, that's all right," the young man said. "Any time." He batted his eyes.

Bennett smiled wanly and left the store. He located an outside phone booth beside a parking lot nearby and found that Montcrieff's was at the far end of Melrose, near Beverly Hills. He drove his car from the parking lot where he'd left it, west in the morning traffic, to Montcrieff's, which was located in a single-story stucco building in an area of decorator shops and craftsman studios. Bennett parked on the street and entered the showroom, a great oblong area in which glass-fronted showcases covered three walls. The cases were filled with masks of every type, and complete animal heads, prominent among them gorillas, bears, dogs, and cats. Hanging in the glass case on the wall farthest from the entrance was an almost exact reproduction of the mask the man who had attacked Bennett had been wearing. The same arched, carefully drawn eyebrows, the same pert turned-up nose, the same full sensual mouth, red lips enticingly open. Two women sat behind a counter, each at a desk, each on the phone, order pads before them. Through a large doorway that opened from the showroom to a workshop in the rear of the building, Bennett could see workers modeling masks, or placing objects in shipping cartons, or painting designs on unfinished clay surfaces before they were placed in a firing oven that stood against the back wall. In this quick glance he did not see any more of the porcelain masks.

The woman closest to him was the first to finish her phone conversation. As soon as she'd hung up, she completed her work on the order form she'd been writing, tore the page off the pad it had been attached to, and carried it to a wire basket set in an opening between the front room and the rear workshop.

"They need two dozen more of the cat heads," she shouted through the opening. "And they need them yesterday."

"Impossible," one of the men in the back room replied.

"They're desperate," the woman said. "But of course they're always desperate." She had bright red hair the color of a fire truck, dressed to hang to her shoulders from a part in the center of her skull. She looked, in her careful makeup, like a woman in her early forties. She smiled a great deal, revealing perfect white teeth that might not have been hers, while her brown eyes semed about to weep. It was difficult to tell whether you were to respond to the eyes or the smile.

"Sorry to have kept you waiting," she said to Bennett, "but certain of our customers have no appreciation of the difficulties we encounter here. They think in order to produce a dozen cat's heads we wave a magic wand and say 'abracadabra' and burn a little incense and there's a dozen cat's heads. Of course that's impossible." The eyes grew sadder and the smile increased. "But," she bravely continued, "no one promised me a rose garden. Or even a rose," she sighed.

"It must be murder," Bennett said sympathetically.

"But enough of my troubles," she said. "How can I help you?"

Bennett pointed toward the porcelain mask in the showcase. "I would really like to own a mask like that," he said.

"Oh, those aren't for sale," she answered quickly. "In fact, that's it, the single and solitary remnant of that stock. We keep it as an example of our work, so we couldn't possibly sell it." She looked at him curiously, at the unshaved face, the casual unpressed clothes. Bennett noted the look.

"I'm with a musical group," he explained. " 'Daylight Savings Time.' "

She looked puzzled but she was not about to drive away the wealthy. One thing she had discovered, working at Montcrieff's, was that the more miserable looking the patrons, the richer they were. The man in front of her, whom she'd thought might be a demented bum, she now held in new respect. A musician! Of course! One of those characters from a rock group! She couldn't recall ever having heard of "Daylite Savings Time," but what would she know? And the reason he wanted that stupid mask was because when he was high on those drugs all those people shot up with, he wanted to wear a mask like that! Probably also a faygalah!

"Let me see, now," she said, her eyes near weeping, her smile broader than ever. "Let me see what we can

90

do about this. You understand why I can't sell you that item? It's our last, practically a museum piece, you might say. Our only copy. You understand?" she begged.

"Oh yes," Bennett told her. He wasn't certain what mental process had brought her to this helpful position, but he was happy to accept it.

"What had you planned to do with the mask?" she asked him, almost afraid what his reply might be.

"I wanted to wear it," Bennett said. "Put it on over my face."

"For your music," she guessed.

"All right!" Bennett enthused.

"The kind you wear was a different order," she said, incomprehensibly. Then, suddenly, her hands flew to her mouth. "Oh my goodness!" she exclaimed. "That's where you saw it!"

Bennett didn't know what she was talking about.

"If you wanted to wear it," she said, "this type of mask can't be worn. They're flat. They're for decoration. They're used in displays. So if it occurred to you to wear it, it's because you saw the picture." Even her eyes began to look pleased.

Bennett pasted a pleasant innocuous smile on his face and hoped she'd continue with her thought.

" 'The Dungeons of Hell County,' " she said, as though that made sense.

" 'The Dungeons of Hell County!' " Bennett repeated enthusiastically.

"The scene in the department store at night," she said, "after everyone has gone home."

"The scene in the department store at night after everyone has gone home," Bennett echoed.

"And the mannequins come to life!" she exclaimed. "It comes before we see them carrying the guns and

91

knives. When they're still friendly and we think they're good and kind because we don't know yet they're under the control of the dungeon master, whose will and orders they're sworn to obey because of the promise they made that in return for a few hours of life each night after the department store was empty, they would turn their personal souls over to the dungeon master, neither expecting or even dreaming what horrible things he would make them commit." It was the first time she'd been animated. Her cheeks were flushed with excitement, her sad eyes glittered with happiness, her smile was real and relaxed. "Several of those mannequins wore masks we made specially for the film and you saw it and remembered it and that's what was on your mind, that's what you were thinking of." She stopped and took a deep breath and looked around as though she expected an ovation from a crowd which might have gathered as she was speaking.

"Fantastic!" Bennett complimented her. "Really fantastic!"

"You saw it on the late show three weeks ago last night," she said, waiting for his corroboration. "Correct?"

"You're too good for this job," Bennett said. "Unless you're the president of this company, you're too good for this job."

Her face flushed with pleasure. "It's just because I happen to like that particular film," she said, suddenly shy. "Normally I wouldn't have that much recall about one of our products. But when we made those masks I wondered what they were for, how they were going to be used, and then we were all invited to the studio to see a preview of the picture and that had never happened to me before, that I was invited to the studio to see a film. There were only twenty of us in the studio theater," she said in wonder. "Imagine that! They ran this film just for the twenty of us in that theater. And when I saw those masks we'd made right here, saw how they were used in that film, it really stunned me. I've never forgotten it. Of course, I've seen many films in studio theaters since then," she added quickly, not wanting to leave Bennett with the impression that a lady her age who lived in Hollywood and worked at Montcrieff's was without friends in the motion-picture industry. "Many films," she said.

"It's always a thrill, though," Bennett said.

"Oh yes," she admitted, beginning to slip back to sad eyes and smiling mouth. "Always a thrill."

"When was the picture made?" Bennett asked.

The answer surprised him.

"Nineteen years ago this month," she said. "When I first came to work here."

Bennett's dream of an immediate connection between mask manufacturer and Sonny vanished.

"Nineteen years?" he repeated. "Are you sure?"

"Oh yes," she said. "Absolutely positive." Sad eyes stared at him reproachfully while her mouth smiled. "We got the order just after I came to work here, and that was nineteen years ago this month." She looked over her shoulder at a calendar which hung on the wall behind her, November illustrated by a long-legged girl dressed in what appeared to be a mince pie with a wedge cut out of the top, giving her an unusual amount of cleavage. "November, just before Thanksgiving. My boss made a joke about it. He said I got the day off almost before I started work." She seemed about to cry, but her smile was wider and braver than ever.

"Is there a mold of the mask that was used in the picture?"

93

"So you might be able to make one for yourself? No, no mold." She shook her head negatively. "In fact I have a distinct memory of how, after the order was delivered to the studio, we destroyed the mold. The studio didn't want us making those masks for anyone else, they wanted them exclusively. So we destroyed the mold." Her left arm extended and she pointed dramatically to the back room. "Back there," she said. "We all gathered round, and there was a man from the studio, no there were two of them, a prop man and a lawyer, and we put the mold on one of the tables, that one I think it was," her arm moved to the left and picked out a table near the kiln, "and my boss took a hammer and he said 'Go with God' and he smashed the mold with a single blow." Remembering, she shook her head in wonder. "It broke into a hundred pieces," she said. "So you see you couldn't make one today from that mold. No way. Because the mold was broken into a hundred pieces."

"Who made the picture?" Bennett asked.

"It was an independent," she said. "I can't even remember the man's name. But it was his first picture. I never heard of him again after that. Would you like his name? Would that help you?" she asked, her expression suggesting that she didn't really have the time to continue further with this conversation, even if he were a terribly rich musician.

"Would you?" Bennett asked. "I'd be very grateful."

The weight of the world on her shoulders, her trembling sigh carried her to an alcove in which filing cabinets stood. "I can only get you the information if the file is under the picture title," she threw over her shoulder, defensively.

"I understand," he reassured her.

She was undecided whether to look under *T* for

8

"Can I borrow this for a while?" Bennett asked. "I want to have a copy made so I can show it to the rest of my group. They don't understand what I've been talking about."

She seemed uncertain.

"I'll have it copied right over there," Bennett said, pointing to a film fan photo shop across the street. "You can watch me go in."

"Well . . ." she said.

When Bennett wanted to be charming, his black eyes softened and his smile warmed and his voice caressed. "Less than an hour," he said.

"Okay," she agreed after the slightest pause. "But I have to have your word, because that's the only picture in the file."

"My solemn word," he swore.

She handed him the photograph.

"I'll be right back," he said, and darted across the street to the film fan shop, where actors ordered copies of photographs, which they autographed and mailed to those who'd written and requested them. Inside, Bennett explained to a young man what he wanted and how important it was to have it immediately, while waving

"The" or *D* for "Dungeons." She began with a file close to the floor, pulling out the gray steel drawer, then walking her fingers across the tops of the folders.

"It's not under *T*," she called back to Bennett.

She slid the drawer shut and selected another, this one close to her waist. She pulled it open, then again walked her fingers across the folders. "Well, aren't you lucky," she said, lifting a folder from the drawer. " 'Dungeons of Hell County,' " she said, bringing the folder to the counter where Bennett waited. She placed it on the counter top with both hands, handling it as though it were a scarce and terribly valuable museum piece. She rested both hands on it, palms down, and held that position for a minute as though praying. "I'm remembering that night when we saw the picture in the studio theater," she explained.

Bennett nodded sympathetically.

She stood there for a moment, her eyes closed. Then, with a shake of her head, eyes opened, she said something that sounded like "well," under her breath, and opened the folder. In it were several sheets of paper which looked like order forms, and a copy of a cancelled check. "Payment," she said, "closing the account." She skimmed through the papers. "The release title of the picture was 'The Dungeons of Hell County.' It had two earlier titles, 'Danger in the West,' and 'These Girls Are Monsters.' " She made a face. "I'm glad the title was changed," she said to Bennett.

"So am I," he agreed.

"The production company was Galley Films," she read from an invoice. "The check was signed for Galley Films by L. George Galley." She seemed pleased with that bit of information, and formed her face into an expression that suggested the information made sense. "And that's all I have," she said. "The delivery address was Paramount Pictures, on Marathon, which is where they shot the picture, rented the space, and that's where we delivered the masks." She closed the folder. "Are they going to be part of your act?" she asked. "I mean, were you planning to use the masks in one of your concerts?"

"That was the idea, yeah," Bennett said.

"Well, I'm sorry I wasn't of more help," she said. "I certainly hope you can locate one or two of the masks, although for the life of me I can't believe any of them are still around."

One of them is, Bennett thought.

"You've been helpful. Thanks," he told her.

"If you use them in a concert I'd certainly appreciate knowing about it," she said as Bennett turned to leave.

"I'll see that you get tickets," he said, stepping out onto Melrose.

He'd started to walk to his car when she caught up with him.

"I forgot to show you this," she said, waving a photograph. "It was in the folder. A publicity still. You can see how well the masks looked."

She handed him a glossy eight-by-ten photograph of a department store interior. In the dim night lighting, Bennett could see what appeared to be the cosmetic section of the store. Glass showcases lined the aisles, and in and on them were bottles and containers and boxes of cosmetics, creams and lotions and perfumes and lipstick and mascaras and eye shadows. In the center of the middle aisle stood a figure, a slight person dressed all in black, black shoes, black slacks, a black turtleneck sweater, and a black knit watch-cap. Whoever it was in the nineteen-year-old photograph was an

96

exact physical double of the man called was wearing a porcelain mask.

"Who's that, do you know?" Bennett to the figure.

"That's the producer," she said. "Th ley."

97

some money rather grandly. He ordered six copies, after being told it was the first one which was expensive, that once the new negative had been made there were no problems, and within thirty minutes he had what he wanted, and returned to Montcrieff's with the original.

"As promised," he told the woman. "And I'm really grateful."

"You won't forget," she said. "If you do use the masks in a concert you'll let me know."

"If I use them in a concert you'll be the first to know," he said.

He drove back downtown. It was nearly four o'clock and he hoped Pinky would have some information for him. He parked in a lot several blocks from the streets he'd been working and walked back to the bus station, where he sat on a bench off to one side and waited for Pinky. It was ten minutes to four, and the waiting room was crowded with travelers. Looking around, Bennett was taken by the number of Oriental people who were there, relaxed adult faces not frightened as he had seen them in Vietnam, the children bright and gay, the war forgotten in the safety of their new environment.

"Slide over," Pinky said. He'd come in through the side door, behind Bennett. Bennett slid over and Pinky sat down beside him.

"Hey," he said, "this Sonny? The guy you wanted me to find out about at the Majestic? I got a couple of things that might be of interest to you." He glanced cautiously around the waiting room, as if perhaps he was being watched or had been followed.

"What's his name?" Bennett asked.

"That's the first thing I inquired into," Pinky said. "His name. I mean, you don't go through life with only the name of Sonny. Am I correct?"

"Correct."

"So I made a few inquiries of people I know who know other people at the Majestic, to find out has this guy Sonny got a name." Pinky's friendly face was very serious. He wanted Bennett to understand that the information he was about to impart hadn't been collected without considerable effort.

"And what were these friends able to pass along to you?" Bennett asked. He'd found out from his first contacts with Pinky that the man couldn't be pushed. He said what he had to say at his own pace.

"These friends researched the matter very carefully," Pinky continued. "They didn't go to the subject of the discussion and say to him, hey what's your name besides Sonny? Nor did they go to him and say how come your name is Sonny, that's not a name that's a nickname, what's your real name? They did none of those things."

"Very wise of them," Bennett dryly commented.

Pinky quickly looked to see if Bennett was serious. "Yes it was," he said sternly. "Very wise of them. Because when you're doing this type of work you can't be too careful. Well, you know that, I don't have to tell you that. Care and what you might call discretion is very very important at this kind of work. Without it the subject gets suspicious and . . ." he whistled through his teeth and his right hand scooted out, "without it the subject disappears."

"Right," Bennett said, restraining his impatience.

"What had to be done, without attracting attention or suspicion, was to get a look at the Majestic register, to see how Sonny had checked in. Since my sources didn't know right away when it was he'd checked in, they therefore needed time to go through the file. What I'm saying is they couldn't just go to October twelfth, let's say, making up a date, you understand, because they didn't know when it was he had signed the register. You understand what I'm saying?"

Bennett said he understood.

"So what they were prepared to do in the enterprise is go through the Majestic's register, going backwards from today, looking for Sonny's real name. You see the error in their plan?" Pinky asked.

"Unless he registered as Sonny they'd never find it," Bennett said.

"Exactly," Pinky said. "Which is what I explained to them when they related to me what it was they were preparing to do. These sources," Pinky said, in a quiet confidential tone, "a couple of them haven't got it all up here." He tapped his temple with a well-kept index finger.

"How'd your sources solve their problem?" Bennett asked.

"They got a hold of his last name from one of the guests, and with that information, they went through the register. His last name is Galley."

Bennett sat up straight.

"His full name is L. George Galley, although for some reason he's called Sonny. He checked into the Majestic four weeks ago. On his register card, under home address, he wrote 'La Jolla, California.' Under business firm he wrote 'Pierce-Arrow Motor Car Company,' so the guy's got a sense of the humorous."

Having completed that part of his explanation, Pinky leaned back on the bench and studied the busy waiting room.

"Did you ever notice how many Oriental people have come to this country since the war in Vietnam?" he asked. "Why's that, do you think?"

"It's safer here," Bennett said.

Pinky raised his thick eyebrows.

"No bombs or cannons or rifles," Bennett said. "You know."

"Oh yeah," Pinky said. "I didn't think of that."

"What else did you find out?" Bennett asked, after Pinky had had time to digest the answer to his question about the Vietnamese.

"Find out?"

"About Sonny," Bennett reminded him. "Listen. Are we here to work, or are you handicapping those goddam horses again?"

"No, no, we're here to work. You paid me for information, you're going to get information. You know my reputation."

"That's why I mentioned the horses," Bennett said.

"Well, to give you a direct answer, no, I wasn't thinking about horses. What I was thinking is, this guy's name cost you the twenty you gave me, so the price for the rest of what I have for you is the other thirty you said the job was worth in your estimation." He looked at Bennett to see if he was pushing it too far. "You understand what I'm saying?"

"Sure, I understand," Bennett said. "But I'll decide how much I owe you after you tell me what you've got."

"That's a funny kind of deal," Pinky said.

Bennett shrugged.

"Well, all right. Here's what's interesting." Pinky leaned forward. "Whatever it is how he makes his living," Pinky said, "he has very funny hours. I been trying to figure what sort of job lets a guy sleep most of the day and work most of the night. I mean, I know about bus drivers and cops and so forth and so on, airline pilots is a good example, but this guy Sonny is no airline pilot, or cop, he's not a doctor or a nurse, so it beats me what the hell he does. You got any ideas on that?"

Bennett shook his head that he had no idea.

"Anyhow, that's the information I got, about these strange hours he keeps. Also he doesn't seem to have friends. Keeps to himself. Doesn't even take advantage of the little niceties they got at the Majestic, even if it is an old broken-down place—like laundry service, never uses it, never uses the valet service to get his clothes cleaned or pressed, you know, things you expect from people." He looked at Bennett, at the unshaven face, the uncombed hair, the wrinkled clothes. "Even you, for Chrissakes, whatever the hell it is you're doing you should take care of yourself. You really look like something the Goodwill wouldn't put their hands on."

"What else did you find out?" Bennett wanted to know. "Besides whether this guy bathes and brushes his teeth."

"Well you don't have to turn mean and spiteful," Pinky said. "I was giving you a constructive criticism about yourself and you get pissed off!"

"What else did you find out?" Bennett repeated.

"Well that's about it," Pinky said, sitting back and crossing one leg over the other. He looked around the waiting room. "I can't get over how many Oriental people are here," he repeated. "And what you said about how come they look so nice and relaxed? That was very observant of you."

"Did you ever work with anyone at Paramount Studios?" Bennett asked.

The question surprised Pinky. "My God," he said, "here we are talking about the displaced people of the world, and how some nations open their arms to them,

103

and you come up with Paramount Pictures. How did you get from Southeast Asia to Paramount?"

Bennett waited for a reply.

"That would depend on what you mean by worked with," Pinky said.

"Had contact with, held book for, you know what I'm talking about."

"You're talking about do I have contact with anyone at Parmount Pictures Company."

"Exactly."

"I might have had such a contact."

"Let's say I owe you thirty and there's another fifty if I'm on the lot talking to a guy in the prop department."

Pinky crinkled his eyes as if he were trying to figure out a puzzle. "Let me see if I understand you," he said. "There's something going down which you're working on but you don't want anybody to know you're on it so you use me to get information, and now you want to get some more information from a person in the prop department at Paramount Studios for which you agree to pay me fifty bucks if I can pull it off in addition to what you already paid me and the thirty you owe me." He stared at Bennett to see if he had it right.

Bennett reached into his pocket for some folded bills and handed Pinky a twenty and a ten. "We're up to date," he said. "Now what about Paramount?"

"I'm not going to con you," Pinky confided. "I'm going to be as honest as them scouts." He waved a ringed hand toward a family who'd just entered the waiting room from the street. The man and woman carried small suitcases, and herded before them twin boys, six or seven years old and wearing Cub Scout uniforms. "I'm going to go over to that phone over there and make a couple of calls and when I come back I'll give you an honest answer whether or not I can help you with the Paramount Studios part of your inquiry. Fair enough?"

Bennett agreed it was fair enough and Pinky walked over to a magazine stand and changed a dollar bill into dimes. Then he leaned into a public phone and began making calls. As soon as he'd dialed the first number he pulled a pencil from one pocket and an old envelope from another, ready to write down names or addresses or phone numbers. He stacked his dimes neatly beside the envelope, a businessman at work. He made four or five calls, speaking quietly and pleasantly to each party, writing quickly on the back of the envelope. Bennett wondered if there were any area in which Pinky hadn't contacts, hadn't friends or acquaintances who owed him something for past favors, for pieces of information similar to what he'd so often dug up for Bennett.

He returned to his seat on the bench beside Bennett, putting his pencil back into his pocket and holding the unused dimes and the envelope in his hand. "I can get you what you need," he said as he sat down. "There is a person who works at the Paramount Studios who would be happy to meet with you in the prop room there, and chat with you for a while, maybe answer questions if that's the purpose of your visit unless you're just a tourist who wants to be shown privately around the lot, that's something I didn't make arrangements for because you didn't ask for that."

"Someone in the prop department is all I need," Bennett said.

Pinky, smiling at his accomplishment, waited to be paid.

"Who do I see?" Bennett asked.

Pinky held out his hand.

"I'm not giving you a nickel until I make sure you're not snowing me," Bennett said. "For all I know I pay you and when I get to Paramount they never heard of me and there's no such person as this guy you claim to have set up for me."

Pinky looked hurt. His body sagged and his smiling mouth drooped; his eyes began to tear.

"Don't bullshit me," Bennett said. "Give me the name. I'll go see the guy. If it works out like we both want it to, then you've got your fifty."

"You must have had a lot of disappointments in your life," Pinky said. "There's a lot of distrust in you, Bennett. I'm not at all sure police work is the ideal job for a person like you. It could give you justification for your suspicious ways, hence it doesn't cure your problem, only continues it." Pleased with his analysis, he waited for a few kind and complimentary words. "Did you know that about yourself?" he asked, when Bennett didn't respond.

"I knew," Bennett said. "My choice of police work as a continuing job has been seriously questioned several times recently." I wonder what Polly'd say if she heard Pinky, he thought. Might break her up to find a snitch who agreed with her. "Who do I see at Paramount?" he asked.

The question jolted Pinky back to the matter at hand. "Lew Miller," he said.

"He in props?" Bennett asked.

"In and out," Pinky said. "He's more important than that. He works props, he works in the office, he works with the union, he's an all around guy, Lew is."

"Friend of yours?" Bennett asked.

"Me and Lew have been through a couple of things together," Pinky confided. "My second wife? Did you know her? She tried to stick me for alimony, and Lew

106

followed her around a little bit until he got some dirt on her so she'd leave me the hell alone. So he's a friend, yeah. Imagine that bitch was fucking three other guys and wanted me to pay her alimony! Christ! Some people have all the nerve." The memory angered him and his face flushed.

"When's Lew Miller expect me?" Bennett asked.

"In the early A.M.," Pinky said. "Them studio guys, they knock off three, four o'clock in the afternoon if they're not shooting, but they're at work in the morning while it's still dark. Crazy goddam business," he muttered. "Hey, Bennett?" he said. "I can see your point, how you gotta be careful, but you understand I also got to protect myself. I should have some of that fifty now. Jesus, what could happen? If there's no such guy at the studio to help you you'll find me and kick me apart, right?"

Bennett dug fifty dollars out of his pocket. "Here," he said. "If Lew Miller's not there you're going to need new teeth."

Pinky pocketed the money. "Count on me," he said.

"Who'd you tell him I was?" Bennett asked.

"I told him you were an independent television and film producer from the Chicago area who needed some advice on budgets and shooting schedules and so forth and so on."

"Me to a *T*," Bennett said.

It was dark when he got home. Polly was in the living room, watching the evening news. He kissed her, then went into the bedroom and stripped off his clothes. He showered, then shaved off the stubble on his face and combed his hair. In the kitchen, he poured himself a Scotch and water, then sat opposite Polly in front of the television. A woman commentator was giving an adverse report on crime in the city, citing the

107

knife-wielding murderer as an example of how matters had gotten out of the control of the police.

"Don't you want a drink?" he asked her.

"Later," she said.

He listened to the commentator. "What bullshit," he said, sipping on his drink.

Polly shrugged. She seemed listless, uninterested in what she was watching.

"Everything all right?" he asked her.

"Oh, yes."

"Sure?"

"Sure."

The commentator completed her remarks without shaking a warning finger into the lens of the studio camera and saying bad dog, and then she faded away and was replaced by a concentration of commercials extolling suppositories, douches, laxatives, and acne cleansers.

"Things are moving right along," Bennett told Polly, midway into the first of the commercial onslaughts.

"That's good," she said.

"Hey?"

She turned to face him.

"What's the matter? Something bothering you? Anything happen today I should know about?" He knew there was a problem, and he hoped it wasn't about their marriage again.

"Later," she said, turning back to the television.

"I really don't particularly care about all these commercials," he said. "I'd much rather talk to my wife over a drink and discuss what we've been doing and thinking since we last saw each other."

"I haven't been doing anything," she said.

"How about thinking?" he asked her. "What have

you been thinking about?" When she didn't reply, he said, "Us?"

Her head and face moved slightly, acknowledging that that might have been what she'd been thinking about.

"Are you still worried about my job?" he asked her quietly.

She didn't look at him. She nodded her head.

"I don't know that I could do anything else. I enjoy my work. It sounds corny but I do."

"It frightens me," she said softly. "I told you I was trying, but it comes across me in waves sometimes. It's like living in a nightmare, where the most awful things happen and you're helpless to prevent them."

"I can't quit," he told her.

"You haven't tried," she said. "Couldn't you take a leave of absence so that you could at least look around? Police work is all you know because it's something you fell into when you got back from Vietnam. You might enjoy something else a lot better. I know I would." She'd been staring at the television screen as she spoke, as though the actors in the commercial were people to whom she was speaking. Now she suddenly turned, her face drawn and somber. "I don't want to not be married to you," she said. "And I don't want you saddled with a job you hate. But I think you ought to find out if there's something else you'd rather do before you're a terribly old man who grumps about what he missed in life. Or before someone kills you while you're a young man doing what you're doing now. I guess I'm repeating myself." She stood up, her hand brushing an unseen web from her face. "I'll be right back," she said.

He heard her in the ktichen, fixing a drink, ice cubes against glass, the splash of a double jigger of whiskey, a quick squirt of club soda, the stirring action of a spoon in the glass filled with ice and liquid. Then she came back into the room and sat down.

"Well?" she asked.

"Let me think about it," he said. "There might be a way."

There wasn't, of course, at least not one he could think of that quickly. First, there was the matter of money. If he were to take a leave of absence, assuming Drang could arrange such a thing, he and Polly would need money to live on while he worried through who he was and where he was and what he really wanted to do with his life. Perhaps she was right, perhaps he was in police work because he hadn't explored anything else. But what else was there? He couldn't imagine himself not being a cop. But neither could he imagine himself not married to Polly.

"Maybe there's a way," he told her again. "We'll see."

She didn't completely believe him, but she was satisfied for the moment that the subject had been discussed and that he'd finally agreed to think about it. It was better than an explosion from him, one of those sudden violent yelling fits he sometimes had, where past rages combined with present frustrations until he angrily stamped about, yelling so forcefully the cords on his neck stood out. She'd learned not to yell back, to let him vent the steam, because as quickly as it happened it was over. She'd often wondered whether he did that at work, whether he suddenly screamed while driving in a patrol cruiser, or yelled at a witness. She guessed not, because if it had happened she imagined she'd have heard about it. She'd never asked him directly because she'd never found the exactly appropriate moment for the question. And Drang had never said anything about it, in the times the three of them were together. She guessed that the seat of the problem was his Vietnam war experience, but that was something he rarely discussed with her, and so she didn't really know. The rages might even have had something to do with his childhood, with the tragedies of the deaths of his mother and his father, but he'd only spoken of that once or twice. She knew more about it from his stepfather, J. D. Cowper, who'd told her of Bennett's father's death, when the boy was only five. And how a year later, J. D. had met Bennett's mother and married her. Even though J. D. had adopted him, Bennett, from some sense of loyalty, had continued to call himself by his dead father's name. Then, only a year or so after her marriage to J. D., Bennett's mother had fallen into a deep depression. She had been undergoing medical treatment but her depression persisted, and Bennett had always believed, deep in his soul, that her drowning was not an accident but a deliberate act of suicide. At times, when Bennett fell into one of his black moods, Polly wondered if perhaps it was a medical problem, something he'd inherited from his mother. She had tried to suggest that one evening, but he'd rejected her notion completely, and stormed from the house in a rage. He had apologized later, when he had returned home, calling his behavior childish and swearing it would never happen again; but please, it was something he wanted to forget, he wanted no further analysis of why he did this or that. Polly had agreed.

She'd expected that, as he rose through the department ranks, his work would become less dangerous. Instead, it had grown more so, and as that happened she began to doubt that their marriage could continue. She was not a woman who could live with the tension of being the wife of a police officer.

111

But she loved him, and knew he loved her.

Maybe his latest promise would help, she thought as they prepared for bed. Maybe he would agree to take an extended leave of absence from the department, time for them to consider another job for him, a satisfying and rewarding job, without the dangers he now faced. And then maybe their marriage would be regenerated, and the growing lapses between them would heal.

She didn't consider where they'd get the money for a year's sabbatical. Perhaps she should have.

9

Bennett drove up to the Paramount auto gate at six-thirty in the morning and took his place in line with the crews, actors and actresses, and studio staff personnel who were being checked onto the lot. When it was Bennett's turn a friendly looking uniformed guard asked his name and his business, thumbed a stack of passes, found one that confirmed Bennett's appointment with Lew Miller, and directed him where to park and how to find the prop department. Bennett followed directions, driving slowly past hospital patients and cowboys, policemen and riffraff, baseball players and space creatures, all hurrying to the sound stages where they were to work that day. He parked in the area the guard had assigned him, and wandered the busy studio streets until he found a sign that said "Prop Department." As he approached an office that fronted a barn-like structure in which props were stored, the door opened and a man stepped out.

"Bennett?" he asked.

"Yeah. Right."

"Lew Miller, come on in."

Bennett followed him into a small, cluttered room in which guns were piled everywhere, rifles and handguns, submachine guns and shotguns, dozens and dozens of them.

"Looks like an arsenal, right?" Miller said. "We're preparing a show with a lot of weapons. We need so damn many weapons I had to rent some, we didn't have the stuff here, and we got about the best selection in the business." He took three shotguns off a chair. "Sit down, it's almost clean. Get you some coffee? It's pretty good."

Bennett sat and agreed he'd like a cup of coffee. Miller pushed aside a stack of old newspapers and reached for an ancient blue coffee pot on a hot plate. Half a dozen ceramic mugs were alongside. Miller's mug said "Chief" on it. He selected "Brain Surgeon" for Bennett, and filled both mugs with coffee.

"Sugar? Fake cream?" he asked.

"Black," Bennett said.

Miller handed Bennett his mug, then sat behind a battered old desk, brushing aside several scripts. He was a lean man with the lined, outdoor face of the cowboy in cigarette ads. Most outstanding about him was his thick snow-white hair, made to appear even whiter by his tanned forehead. His hands, when he picked up his mug of coffee, looked lean and tough.

"Pinky tells me you're doing a show in Chicago," he said.

"Preparing it," Bennett said. "Trying to get everything together."

"Seems impossible, doesn't it?" Miller smiled, and sipped at the hot coffee.

"One of the things we're trying to get into the film," Bennett said, trying to sound like someone who knew what he was talking about, "is what I suppose you'd call complete authenticity. Incidentally, did Pinky tell you what the film's about?"

114

Still smiling, Miller shook his head that Pinky hadn't told him. "You know Pinky," he said. "He just calls you and says 'Hey, I want you to do this friend of mine a favor,' and you do it. That Pinky," he said wonderingly.

"It's a semidocumentary," Bennett said. "We've got what I think is a good story, a horror story, you know, very commercial, but the gimmick is how we use masks. Which is where I need your help, where I'd like to pick your brain. Is that your department? That's how green I am, this is my first feature, I'm not even sure I'm bothering the right guy."

"I'd consider masks props," Miller said. "I know a couple of folks over in wardrobe who'd think that was their department, but no, I'd consider masks to be props."

"Yeah, well, you see?" Bennett said. "That's how little I know."

"How can I help you?" Miller asked.

"Well, a funny thing happened," Bennett began. "We'd been working on this thing, oh, nearly a year, I'd guess, you know, getting the script the way we wanted it, checking the availability of actors, talking to our money guys, you know."

"Oh yeah," Miller agreed, sadly shaking his mane of white hair as though they were discussing a Greek tragedy. "Oh man, do I know."

"Then a couple of weeks ago, I think it was, a month, maybe, I'm in bed with my wife, we're watching the late news, we're ready to go to sleep, and there's a teaser for this movie the station's going to run later that night, and there're these masks. I'd never seen them before. Just beautiful. Well, you won't believe this: I stayed up until three o'clock in the morning to see the picture."

" 'The Dungeons of Hell County,' right?" Miller said, very sure of himself.

Bennett expressed surprise. "Right," he agreed. "How'd you know?"

"I propped that show," Miller said. "And it was on TV here too, in L.A., week or so ago. I'd forgotten about it, it was a real turkey. . . ."

"Yeah, right," Bennett agreed. "Terrible show."

"But when I watched it I was real pleased with the way those masks worked out. We had them made for the picture," he told Bennett. "Special order. Scare the hell out of you, don't they?"

"Absolutely," Bennett said, remembering the way his attacker had looked, the knife slashing at Bennett's throat, while the impassive porcelain face stared. "Scare the hell out of you."

"The gag really worked," Miller said. "I'd forgotten about it," he repeated. "You know, you make so many pictures you forget some of them. Not just the turkeys, some of the good ones, too. Some of the turkeys you remember because they were so terrible, you know, really crap. 'The Dungeons of Hell County,' that was lousy, but not so bad you remember it. That's why it surprised me when I saw it on TV the other week. And they played it in Chicago, too? Son of a bitch." He finished his coffee and rose from his chair. "How's your coffee?" he asked. "Here, I'll warm it up for you." He lifted the coffee pot off the warming plate and refilled Bennett's mug, then his own, and replaced the pot. "I don't suppose there's a picture ever been made that hasn't been on TV or will be on TV," he mused as he sat down behind his desk. "It doesn't matter how lousy, they'll put the worst piece of crap in a package with a box-office smash so the studio can recoup their money. If the stations want the smash they've got to take the turkey. Show biz," he said.

"Who directed 'Dungeons?' " Bennett asked.

"Larry Marple, I think. He died about a year after we shot the thing. Nice guy. Old timer. Knew all the tricks. I think we shot the picture in three weeks, locations, special effects, wrapped the whole damn thing in three weeks. They take three weeks now to make up their minds where to put the camera, some of these new guys. Some of these new kids, that show that we did in three weeks? It would take a year and cost forty million. Some show biz," he said. He moved his coffee mug angrily, using it to push aside a sheet on which he'd been figuring costs on one of the scripts on his desk.

"What sort of man was the producer? What's his name? Galley?" Bennett asked.

"L. George?" Miller asked, smiling. "Pretty nice guy. Little guy. You know him?"

Bennett said he didn't.

"Pretty nice little guy. He liked practical jokes. Like he'd put on one of the masks and he'd stand behind a flat, and when one of the girls walked past he'd jump out and yell 'boo,' you know, kidding. And they'd scream like he'd scared them. It kept the set relaxed. Pretty nice little guy," Miller said.

"How old a man was he?"

"L. George? He was a real young guy. Lemme see, we made that picture . . . must be twenty years ago. That's one of the things that was so funny about L. George. I mean, here's a real young guy, maybe twenty-four, twenty-five years old, he's not only the producer of the movie, his name's L. George, for Chrissakes. Can you imagine calling a twenty-four-,

117

twenty-five-year-old kid L. George?. It used to crack me up."

"Is he still around?" Bennett asked. "I'd like to talk to him about some projects."

Miller looked startled. "L. George?" he said. "I think he died."

"Recently?"

"Let me see," Miller said. Then, apologetically, "I'm getting to the age where I can't remember who's dead and who's alive. I'll think someone's dead and meet them at the supermarket, or I'll run into a lady and say give my best to Bert, who's her husband, and she looks at me like I'm not all there and says Bert's dead, you were at the funeral." He rubbed his tough hand across his face. "I'd have to admit I'm not sure about L. George—but I think I read he died. But don't count on me. He could be dead or he could just as easily be alive and kicking. But it seems to me he's dead."

"Well, I'll ask around," Bennett said.

"They might know at the Motion Picture Academy," Miller suggested. "They keep track of everyone in the business."

Bennett thanked him and finished his coffee. "By the way," he said, almost as if it were an afterthought. "I'd like to take one of those masks back with me, show my crew what fine work you guys did. Have you got any of them around?"

"I doubt it," Miller said. "I mean that was almost twenty years ago when we did that show. As you can see," he laughed, his arm taking in the room, "we don't throw very much stuff away, but twenty years. . . ."

"I'd really like to take one back with me," Bennett said. "I'll be happy to pay for it."

Miller looked doubtful. His hand wiped at his face

once again. "Well," he said, "I could look through the index, see if they're still here."

"I'd appreciate it."

Miller swung around in his chair, which noisily protested as he turned, and pulled open the middle drawer of a dented steel filing cabinet that was guarded by piles of guns and ammunition cases. He quickly ran through the drawer, then pulled something out, and held it up for Bennett to see.

"Original purchase order," he explained. He studied it. "We had twenty of those masks made, at Montcrieff's, over on Melrose. We used twelve in the picture; the remainder were back-ups, if the others got busted or chipped, or the director had a stunt he wanted to do where we needed working doubles, you know."

Bennett nodded that he knew, although he didn't.

Miller replaced the purchase order in the file and scrounged through the other papers. "Here's a request from someone who wanted to use the masks in a musical, but they needed a hundred of them for all the dancers so they didn't use them. I think I remember they changed the number to a puberty dance or something like that and didn't use masks at all, just lots of feathers and that sort of crap someone over in wardrobe made up." He looked at Bennett. "You know how them wardrobe people are," he said, resting a hand on his hip.

Bennett nodded, keeping the conspiracy alive.

Miller continued his search, studying each sheet of paper in the file. "Storage," he said, "took them out of there," his head nodded toward the barn-like building behind the office, "and put them in storage." He looked up at Bennett. "That's usually before they sell stuff, or give it away," he said. "Although I don't know many times they ever gave anything away around here. Around here they wouldn't give away shit. They sell everything around here. That's why I had to rent so many of these weapons. We used to have enough stuff here so I could outfit a cavalry troup—period stuff, you know—and some new bosses came in, lawyers and accountants, and they see this stuff just hanging around in there," the head nodded toward the storage area, "and they can't see a damn thing beyond the piece of paper they've got in their hands, they don't know every picture's different. So they see we're not using some stuff they sell it, that's why I had to rent all these weapons. Some show biz," he grunted.

"That what happened to the masks?" Bennett asked. "Were they sold?"

Miller went back to the file. "Into storage," he repeated. "Here's storage bills," he looked at Bennett again. "There was room here," he complained, "they've got the room, for Chrissakes, and they pull them out of here where it doesn't cost a nickel, and put them in storage, and here's the bills they had to pay." He waved a couple of invoices.

"Are they still in storage?" Bennett asked patiently.

Miller looked back into the file. "Nope," he said. "They're not in storage." He looked at the next piece of paper. "Ah-hah," he said. "Here's what might probably help you. Bill of sale. Sixteen masks."

"Didn't you say twenty were made?" Bennett asked.

"Right. Montcrieff's made twenty of them."

"Then four are missing?"

"Might be. Or we might have broken them when we shot the picture. We probably broke them, and the studio sold the remaining sixteen."

"Is there any way of finding out for sure?" Bennett asked.

Miller looked at him with growing suspicion. "What the hell difference would it make?" he asked. "You just wanted one of them to take back to your guys in Chicago, isn't that right?"

"Yeah, right."

"Then what the hell difference does it make did we bust four of them while we were making this turkey twenty years ago?"

"Well," Bennett explained, "I'll have to tell you the truth."

Miller waited for Bennett to tell him the truth.

"I wanted to use them in my picture," Bennett confessed. "I wanted my picture to have a really unique and different look, and if some of them are still around and someone else's got them, it'll look like I'm copying, you know? I mean, I don't mind that they were in 'Dungeons,' that's an old film, but I sure wouldn't want to spend money getting them for my brand new picture and then there's four of them that show up in another guy's film. You've got to admit they're unique. Even if you were the one who thought of the gag, you got to admit they're unique, there's no question of it in my mind."

Miller accepted the compliment. He thoughtfully leaned back in the chair. "I see what you mean," he said.

"Is there any way you can find out if those four were broken while you were shooting," Bennett asked.

"Just my memory," Miller said. "I'll just have to try and remember."

"I'd appreciate it," Bennett said. Then, casually: "Who were the sixteen masks sold to?"

Miller looked at the bill of sale. "Well, for Chrissakes," he said.

"Someone you know?" Bennett asked.

121

"Charlie Oliver," Miller said. "You know Charlie?"

" 'Fraid not," Bennett answered. "Who is he?"

"A real character," Miller said. "Fine man. My God, Charlie Oliver must be close to eighty by now." He looked back at the bill of sale, smiling. "Charlie Oliver," he said, bemused. "I'll be damned."

"Do you suppose he'd sell me one of the masks?"

"If he still has them, you mean? I don't know why the hell not. But you never know with Charlie. He's a weird one. You never could outguess what Charlie Oliver was going to do."

"Where do I find him?" Bennett asked.

"He had an office here on the lot for years," Miller said. "But then they got so busy here and he hadn't done a picture in a hell of a long time, so he gave up the office." He'd closed the folder and opened a seedy-looking telephone book he kept in the middle desk drawer. "Lessee," he muttered, turning worn and soiled pages. "You know how long I've had this phone book? Since before we made 'Dungeons.' Imagine that!" He was a man who felt wonder at simple things and complained about more complicated ones.

"What'd he do?" Bennett asked. "This Charlie Oliver?"

"Producer," Miller replied. "The old-fashioned kind. Put the deal together, picked the property, hired the writer, got the stars, raised the money, set the distribution, oversaw the publicity campaign, the whole schmeer. There's not a lot of them around any more. He was like football used to be, when eleven guys played the full sixty minutes. Now there's a different guy for each little job. Charlie Oliver was like football used to be. He did it all. Now there's fifty guys tripping over each other to get to production meetings where nothing's decided. Or if it is, it's wrong."

122

"Seems to me there's still some guys like Charlie Oliver around," Bennett said, wondering why he was defending a business he knew nothing about.

"Oh well yeah," Miller quickly agreed. He'd been agreeing for so many years it would have been impossible for him to change now. "Here you go," he said, having found what he was looking for. "I've got the address for Charlie Oliver. Old Bel Air. East Gate, where the money is. Ten Eight Oh Five Corsicana." He looked up. "That old place must be worth twelve million now, if Charlie's still got it. I bet he has. He always was a wise old bird. I don't have a phone number," he apologized.

"That's all right," Bennett reassured him. "I'll wander by, maybe he's home. East Gate, did you say?"

"Drive out Sunset," Miller said. "East Gate is after you go through Beverly Hills. It's marked, you can't miss it. Turn right into Bel Air, ask anyone you see, the place is crawling with gardeners, ask any one of them for Corsicana. Charlie's house is a big old place on about half a million acres of lawn, stone house, curved driveway, you'll find it."

"Well, thanks," Bennett said. "I appreciate your help."

"How long you going to be in town?" Miller asked as he stood up.

Bennett shrugged. "Maybe the end of the week," he said. He stuck out his right hand and Miller shook it. "I'll call you tomorrow and let you know how I did," he said. "And maybe you'll remember what might have happened to the other four masks."

"Oh yeah, right," Miller agreed. "I'll give it a go." He tapped his temple with his forefinger. "Start up the old computer."

Miller walked him back to his car, and Bennett drove off the lot. As he was about to turn onto Melrose he heard a horn honking, and saw Drang parked on the opposite side of the street. Bennett waved.

Drang stuck his head out of the window and yelled, "Follow me."

Bennett did, to a shopping center a few blocks away, nearly deserted at this early hour. He parked alongside Drang, who got out of his car and walked into a coffee shop. Bennett followed and joined Drang at a back table.

"What in hell are you doing in a movie studio?" Drang asked.

"One thing led to another," Bennett replied. "I don't know who it was that said it, but it's a truism that you never know where the path of life will take you."

A waitress arrived before Drang could stick his thumbs in Bennett's eyes, or otherwise vent his anger.

"Isn't this early for you?" Bennett asked. "And how'd you know where I was?"

"Polly told me. I called the house."

"Ah-hah," Bennett said.

They ordered breakfast. The waitress brought them coffee, and when she'd gone Drang repeated his question. "How did you get from skid row to Paramount?" he asked.

Bennett told him about the masks, how they'd taken him from a downtown department-store window dresser to Montcrieff's to the studio prop department.

Drang made a disagreeable noise in his throat.

"Why'd you want to see me?" Bennett asked.

"Sonny's gone," Drang said.

"What?"

"I had the Majestic under surveillance, but no sign of Sonny. So I sent Sean inside. No cover, he was a cop looking for someone and he had the man's name, Sonny, and he knew this Sonny had been staying at the Majestic, so he asked the night clerk to ring up this Sonny on the phone and tell him someone wanted to ask him a few questions."

"Night clerk's name is Francis," Bennett interjected.

"Francis. All right, Francis looks in his book and he says to Sean, the man you want to talk to checked out of here. He's no longer a guest."

"When'd he check out?"

"Last night. Eight P.M. Sean said he'd like to examine the room, if this—Francis, that his name?—didn't mind. Francis says it would be his pleasure, he's always been cooperative with the police department, and he took Sean up to an empty room, scrubbed clean, or as clean as they get the rooms at the Majestic. No one there. Empty."

Bennett thought about it. "He couldn't have just moved to another room?"

Drang shook his head. "Sean asked to see the check-out slip. Paid cash. Gone. Slid right past the surveillance team."

"Son-of-a-bitch," Bennett muttered. "We've got a crazy loose."

10

The waitress brought their food. They ate silently.

"Have you a last name for him?" Drang asked, after he'd picked at his food.

"L. George Galley," Bennett said. "At least that's the information I've gotten." He swallowed a forkful of eggs.

"Did you get an address? Somewhere he might be now that he's left the Majestic?"

Bennett shook his head. "When I was at the studio asking about those masks, I was told the picture in which they were used, a turkey called 'The Dungeons of Hell County,' I was told that the producer of that picture was a man named L. George Galley."

"The same one?" Drang asked, leaning forward.

Bennett shrugged. "The picture was produced nearly twenty years ago," he said.

"Where's L. George Galley now?" Drang asked.

"Dead."

Drang stared at Bennett. "You're not making a hell of a lot of sense," he said.

Bennett agreed.

"There's a mistake somewhere," Drang said. "There's got to be." He tried some more food, thinking. "I'll put out an A.P.B. on L. George Galley, and we'll see what turns up," he said. "The people at the studio," he continued after a moment. "The ones you talked to. They know you're a cop?"

Bennett shook his head no.

"Keep it that way," Drang said. "You keep doing whatever it is you're doing. I'll get the department busy, and we'll see if we can't make some sense out of this."

Bennett agreed.

Drang paid the check, and they drove off, Drang to downtown Los Angeles, and Bennett west on Sunset toward Bel Air. He drove through Beverly Hills, passing the pink stucco Beverly Hills Hotel just as three limousines crossed in front of him to enter the hotel driveway. He drove through Holmby Hills, where great estates fronted on a winding thoroughfare so thickly trafficked that Rolls-Royces impatiently waited in their driveways for a kindly passing motorist in a bruised fifteen-year-old Volkswagen to stop and let them regally enter the traffic flow. At the eastern edge of Westwood, before the university towers of UCLA became visible, Bennett turned into the east gate of Bel Air, the original and only gate before developers crowded small houses onto hilly pristine streets, making middle and west gates necessary. Gardeners' trucks were everywhere, and lawn mowers roared as acres of unnaturally green grass fell to superior firepower. Bennett located Corsicana, which, like all the other streets in this section of Bel Air, was a two-lane asphalt road lined on either side by tall hedges and trees that provided some modicum of privacy to the great homes trying to hide behind them. Number 10805 was one of these homes, built on a rise and facing southeast, the early sun reflecting off the beveled-glass windows that helped it resemble a French chateau. A neat forest-green van was parked in the curved drive near the front entrance, "Triple AAA Weatherproofing, EST. 1975" stenciled on the side. As Bennett drove onto the property and parked along the side of the drive, a young man, uniformed in a forest-green jumpsuit on which "AAA" was emblazoned in pink Day-Glo letters, stepped out the front door, spoke to someone within the house, then smartly turned and marched toward his van. When he saw Bennett he smiled broadly, even white teeth highlighted by the sun, and snapped off a quasimilitary two-fingered salute. Bennett returned the gesture and waited until the van had driven away before stepping out of his car.

He wasn't able to see whoever it was the weatherproofing man had been talking to; the person stood inside the open door, waiting.

"Good morning," Bennett called.

An old man stepped out into the sun. He looked dehydrated, with only small amounts of flesh tightly covering his skeleton. His head was too big for his body, or such was the illusion, since it was a large head, with a high broad forehead. Dark eyes were sunken in the skull, and the skin was pale. The old man was dressed in chino slacks and a Hawaiian overshirt that depicted a pretty girl on a surfboard riding a wave about to break over a palm tree, which by some error in perspective appeared to be growing in mid-ocean.

"Good morning, good morning," the old man replied brightly, as though he might break into song.

"What a day," Bennett said as he approached.

"Glorious," the old man agreed.

"If it's not too early, I'd like to know if Mr. Oliver could talk to me for a minute or two. My name's Bennett, Fred Bennett, I'm out here from Chicago, where

128

I'm getting ready to shoot a film, and if he's available I have a question or two to pose to him."

"You like decaffeinated coffee?" the old man asked.

"Sure. Fine," Bennett said.

"I hate it," the old man said, dark eyes staring out angrily. "Doctor says no caffeine. Can you imagine that? No caffeine!"

"Do you miss it?" Bennett asked.

"There's a couple of people here in town who're still alive that I've known, hell, a long time, and if they were my worst enemies, had been my worst enemies through all the years I'd known them, I wouldn't give the poor sons-of-bitches decaffeinated coffee. It's punishment, that's what it is. The manufacturer claims it tastes the same as coffee. Well, the manufacturer is either a liar or has lost the use of his taste faculties." In his anger he'd begun to breathe heavily, which made the surf roll dangerously, tilting the young woman's surfboard until it seemed she'd crash into the palm tree. "But I'll make you some if you want. Me, I'm going to have a cup of real honest-to-God coffee and that doctor can shove it for all I care."

Bennett tried to smile agreeably.

"I'm the person you're looking for," the old man said. "Charlie Oliver. Come on in. How'd you find out about me?"

Bennett stepped into a cool, quiet house. In the distance he could hear the soft ticking of a grandfather clock. He was in a reception area, a large round chamber with doors leading off it like wheel spokes, connected to the second story of the house by a wide, gently curved staircase. Charlie Oliver walked quickly through the room, with Bennett following, and pushed open a door behind the staircase. Bennett stopped, surprised. They had entered a pale green room filled with

129

orchids, a humid room with one wall of glass, through which a long sweeping lawn could be seen. Large, pale green bamboo chairs were placed on either side of a glass-topped table. Charlie Oliver gestured toward the chairs.

"Sit down," he said. "You really want decaffeinated coffee?" he asked.

"I'll have whatever you're having," Bennett said as he sat. "Are all of these orchids?" he asked.

"Every damn one," Charlie Oliver said proudly. "If you had a month I could name them for you in Latin, and where they're from originally—Africa; South America; Pomona, California—exotic places like that. I could show you how I've even grown some of them from seed, which is damn near impossible to do, except I did it." He walked over to a door at the side of the room, opened it, and yelled: "Coffee, Eileen, and don't argue with me about it, because I've got a guest and he's not going to drink any of that damn decaffeinated stuff you've been pushing." He returned grinning, and sat in a chair across the table from Bennett. "You've got to make your position clear," he said.

There was a sudden loud noise, Bennett couldn't be sure what it was; and then a girl appeared in the doorway, a child, nine or ten years old, wearing jeans and a checkered shirt, long blonde hair hanging to her shoulders.

"You're not supposed to have coffee," she said sternly. "Coffee is a no-no for you."

"Come here," Charlie Oliver said.

The girl walked over to him. He leaned forward and kissed her on the top of her head. "Say hello to Mr. Bennett," he said. "My granddaughter," he said to Bennett. "Eileen."

"No coffee," Eileen warned her grandfather. "How

do you do," she said to Bennett. "You can have coffee, unless it's against your doctor's instructions."

"How do you do," Bennett said. "I'll have whatever your grandfather's having. Whatever's the least amount of trouble."

"Trouble is not the issue," Eileen said. "The issue is whether he can con me into serving him coffee just because you dropped in to visit with him." She turned to her grandfather and said severely, "No coffee. I'd appreciate having a grandfather for as long as possible."

"Yes, dear," Charlie Oliver said meekly.

She marched back into the kitchen. Charlie Oliver sighed. "She's just as bossy as her mother was," he said. "My daugther Gwen. She died. Was killed. Young woman. Beautiful. The grieving widower remarried six months later, which I suppose is all right. I got custody of my granddaughter. Livens the place up, I'll say that for it."

"Beautiful child," Bennett said.

"Yes indeed," the old man said fondly. "Yes indeed." Then, noticing that dots of perspiration had appeared on Bennett's forehead, he said: "Too hot in here for you?"

"No, not at all. Just takes a couple of minutes to get acclimated."

"What can I do for you?" Charlie Oliver asked.

"I'm making a picture in Chicago," Bennett began.

"You know Alan Forbes?" Charlie Oliver interrupted.

"No," Bennett said.

"He makes pictures in Chicago. Used to, anyway. Maybe he doesn't any more. Go on, sorry I interrupted you."

"I'm preparing a picture, a documentary," Bennett said.

131

"That's why you wouldn't know Alan Forbes," the old man said. "He did fiction. Documentary's almost like another line of work. You agree with that?"

"I'd have to agree," Bennett agreed.

"Go ahead."

"There's some stuff in it about masks," Bennett continued.

"Lew Miller, am I right?" the old man asked, the sunken eyes bright. "That piece of crap 'Dungeons,' whatever it was called, used those masks and I bought them and Lew Miller told you that and you're here to talk to me about those masks." He saw the astonished look on Bennett's face. "Sorry," he said. "I'm used to working fast. Don't mean to be impolite."

Eileen appeared, carrying two delicate cups of decaffeinated coffee on a tray on which a creamer and a bowl of sugar also sat. She placed the tray between the men on the glass-topped table.

"Here you are," she said. "Would someone like some toast?" She faced her grandfather. "Have you eaten your breakfast?" she asked.

"Oh yeah, sure."

She didn't believe him. "What'd you eat?" she demanded.

"Uh, that cereal, what-do-you-call-it? Wispies, or something like that. I had a bowl of the stuff." He saw that Bennett was watching. "Did you eat your breakfast?" he mimicked. "I tell you, Eileen, some mornings you're just too much."

Eileen faced Bennett. "My grandfather," she said, "is not well, and there're certain things he must eat, and there're certain things he must not eat. Now, you would expect that when a man got to be my grandfather's age, he'd have grown the brains to know how to take care of himself. Well, my grandfather doesn't always do what he says he did. An example is right now." She turned to her grandfather, who was grinning broadly, exposing pink gums and old yellowing teeth. "When Mr. Bennett is finished talking to you you're going to eat your breakfast."

"Yes, Eileen," he said. "Thank you, dear."

She kissed him and he hugged her to him.

"You have to take care of yourself," she said softly. Then she kissed him again and left the room. The old man's eyes were moist. "Oh I wish her grandmother had been alive to know that child." He blew his nose on a wilted paper napkin.

"The masks," Bennett reminded Charlie Oliver. "You're absolutely right, that's why I'm here. Lew Miller told me you bought sixteen of them."

"Correct," Charlie Oliver agreed, stuffing the napkin in his pocket. "Lew says there were twenty in the original order, but four of them got lost or broken, he couldn't remember; so I figured I could make do with the sixteen."

"I'd like to see them," Bennett said. "I've seen them on the screen, but never close up. I think they're something I can use in my picture."

The old man frowned, and rubbed his knuckle nervously across his mouth. "Well," he said, "I don't think that can be arranged. You see, I bought them because of a picture I was going to do, but they lay around and then I got sick. The picture was delayed, and finally my option on the property expired and I really didn't feel well enough to pick it up again." He'd dropped his voice so his granddaughter couldn't hear him. "So I got rid of all the stuff I'd gathered."

"Did you sell the masks to someone?" Bennett asked.

"Well, as a matter of fact I can't really answer that

133

question. You see, the masks were part of a whole bunch of the kind of junk you collect when you're going to do a picture. Scripts, reference material, props, stills, a million and one things you gather over the years. But hell, I don't have to explain that to you, you're in the middle of the process right now."

"Yeah, right," Bennett said. "That's what I meant. What happened to all that material?"

"I don't really know," the old man said. "Things disappear. Books get swiped or returned, pictures get filed somewhere and no one sees them for fifty years. The masks? They're what you're interested in, but I really don't know what happened to them. Only thing I can tell you is that I'd opened an office at a little joint, Pyramid Studios. When I got sick I told Franny Harris to close things up. She might know what happened to the masks. You want to talk to her? I'll call her and tell her you're on your way, if it's that important."

"I'd appreciate it," Bennett said. "You know how it is, you get your mind set on something, it's hard to just drop the matter unless you're absolutely sure it's hopeless."

"Oh yeah, I understand," Charlie Oliver said. "My daughter was like that. Even more compulsive about things. Couldn't let them go. Hung in there, like . . ." he stopped talking and shook his head in anguish at the memory.

"You said she'd been killed," Bennett said. "An auto accident?"

The old man looked up as though he hadn't heard, a puzzled expression on his face.

"Auto accident?" he repeated. "No, Gwen wasn't killed in an automobile accident. Gwen was murdered."

Bennett felt his stomach knot.

"I'm sorry."

134

"Yeah. Well, the police never did find the guilty party, so my daughter's murderer is still roaming around loose." The old man reached into his rear trouser pocket and pulled out the paper napkin. He blew his nose again, then dabbed at the corners of his eyes. "Terrible thing," he said. "Terrible, terrible thing."

"When did this happen?" Bennett asked.

"Just before I took sick," Charlie Oliver said. "Gwen's death just about did me in. Funny, when my wife died, just after Gwen was born, it wasn't as bad. Funny."

"When did Gwen die?" Bennett replied.

"Year and a half, two years ago," the old man said. "And six months later the widower had remarried." There was an accusing edge to his voice. Bennett wondered if Charlie Oliver thought his ex-son-in-law had had something to do with Gwen's death.

"What was your daughter's married name?"

"Gwen Thompson," Charlie Oliver said. "Mrs. Salvatore Thompson."

Bennett remembered the name, but couldn't recall the circumstances of the case.

"I'll see if Franny's available," Charlie Oliver said, reaching for a telephone nearly buried between banks of orchids arranged on a baker's rack against the wall behind him. "What the hell's her number?" he muttered to himself as he arranged the phone on the glass-topped table. He squinted his eyes closed, pushing the sockets even deeper. "Oh yeah." He lifted the phone and pressed numbers. Bennett could hear the melodic nonsong of the dial tones. "Franny?" Charlie Oliver said, "Good morning, sweetheart. How do you feel today?" He listened, smiling. "That's good. Listen, darling, you remember those masks? The porcelain

135

ones we were going to use?" He listened once more. "Exactly. I think there were sixteen of them. Yes. I'm calling you from home. There's a gentleman here with me from Chicago who's making a documentary movie back there who's interested in the masks. He's even willing to pay us for them. Have you any Idea where they are?" He turned to Bennett. "She's looking," he said. "She sort of remembers them. Marvelous woman. It seems like she was with me forever. She still works part-time occasionally. Well, you can understand that. A woman works all her adult life, it's the same as with a man, retirement is like buying a ticket on a death train, next stop oblivion. Ahh, she's back." He listened again. Then, "She doesn't remember offhand where they are. She sold some stuff, she gave some stuff away, she stored some of the junk. Would you like to go over to her place and talk to her?"

"I'd be obliged," Bennett said. "If it's not putting her out."

"This gentleman could come by your place," Charlie Oliver said into the phone. "Then if you want stuff dragged around that's in your garage, he can do it for you." He looked to Bennett for confirmation. Bennett nodded. "No, he'll help. You shouldn't be lifting boxes and shoving stuff around. Thank you. Maybe one day soon we could have lunch, the two of us. No no no, I'm feeling in top shape. It would be nice to have lunch and talk. We'll even have a bottle of your favorite wine. Yes. I'll call you. This week or next. Thank you, sweetheart. Yes, you know damn well you're my only and true love and always have been, ever since I was a little teeny child and you were a mature woman." Franny said something in reply and Charlie Oliver laughed. "I only wish I could," he said. " 'Bye."

"Marvelous woman," he told Bennett when he'd hung up the phone. "My God, the times we've shared."

"Can she help me?" Bennett asked.

"She thinks she might be able to. She wants a couple of hours to straighten things out at her place. Women," he said. "God love them all. What she wants is time to get herself made up and straighten her house, in which," he said in awe, "you could really eat off the floor."

"That's fine," Bennett said. "Where does she live?"

"You remember the gate you came in, when you entered Bel Air? Well, you go out that gate, it runs into Beverly Glen, you go south past Wilshire, it's on a little street runs into Beverly Glen—2023 South Berwin. Nice little house. She's had it for years."

Bennett wrote down all the information on a note pad, thanked Charlie Oliver, asked to have his best wishes relayed to Charlie's granddaughter Eileen, and departed. Outside, with nearly two hours to spend before meeting Franny Harris, he decided to call on J. D. Cowper, his stepfather. The most recent confrontations with Polly had made him increasingly uneasy about the future of his marriage, and J. D. was one of the few people in the world he could talk to about it.

He had no idea how the move would complicate his life, instead of easing it.

11

Because of his appearance, J. D. Cowper was usually mistaken for a good old country boy, a mountain of innocence who was a ready target for the fast con or the hard-nosed business man. J. D. was large and overweight, his face an improbable assembly of play-dough, nose and cheeks stuck on, warm brown eyes peering out through wrinkles caused less by gravity than by laughter and exposure to wind and sun. His teeth were crooked, and when he smiled you just knew he could be taken, if that was your purpose. His clothes were expensive and well tailored, but looked inexpensive and uncared for. He was a good and decent man to those close to him, and a ruthlessly cold fish to his enemies. He was wealthy but didn't discuss where his money had come from; and whatever his business, he kept it to himself.

J. D. Cowper lived on nine and a half acres of well-manicured land behind the high walls of a community called Arluria, which lay in the hills above Beverly and Cheviot and Bel Air. This country boy turned millionaire lived cheek by jowl with bankers and oil company executives and rock stars and insurance magnates, homey folks who'd selected Arluria as the site of their dream houses because they liked the privacy guaranteed by five-acre-mimimum lots and high stone walls. The only entry to the encampment was by way of guarded gates on the north and the south. J. D. Cowper lived on the highest knoll, in an early California-style ranch home larger than most early California ranches. He lived there with his third wife, Candice, twenty years his junior, and their three children, J. D. Jr., Borden, and Clint.

Bennett was stopped at the south gate by a uniformed guard with steel eyes and a prominently displayed sidearm. Bennett identified himself and who he expected to visit within the compound then waited in front of the closed gate while the guard entered a booth that straddled the road and made a phone call from behind the safety of bullet-proof glass. When he'd relayed Bennett's message and received his instructions, the guard opened the gate and Bennett drove through onto what always seemed to be a smoother road surface than any he'd ever driven before. His car glided: there were no bumps or potholes, only a smoothly winding road that now and then passed a large residence of surpassing beauty. Each of the homes in Arluria had been designed and built by the finest artisans. No two were alike, and they'd been placed in the hills like jewels without changing the shape of the land they occupied.

As Bennett drove up the private lane to J. D.'s house he saw his stepfather standing in the open doorway waiting for him.

"This is a treat," J. D. hollered as Bennett got out of his car. "Unless the reason you're here is some dread matter has come up and you're trying to escape or somesuch."

" 'Morning, J. D.," Bennett said, embracing him. "How are you feeling?"

"First rate, tip-top, you choose the verbiage," J. D. said. "Come on into the house, Elizabeth'll make us some breakfast or mid-morning snack or whatever to hell them things is called that you eat at this time of the day."

Bennett followed him into the house. As they walked through living room, library, dining room, butler's pantry, kitchen, and breakfast room, Bennett said, "Do you really need this much space?"

"Keeps my claustrophobia under wraps," J. D. said. "You just missed your brothers. They left for school not twenty minutes ago. And Candice drove off half a second before they called from the gate to say you was here. Did you pass her?"

Bennett said he hadn't.

"She has a ballet class three mornings a week," J. D. said. "I never knew a person kept herself as busy and occupied as Candice. But enough of that. Tell me, is this an official visit? I done something the department wants to grill me on and so they got a soft spot in their hearts and sent my own kid to ask me the questions?"

"Not official," Bennett said.

" 'Morning, Mr. Bennett," Elizabeth said as they entered the kitchen. She was a tall, slender black woman with a handsome Indian–African face. "What can I get you?"

"He'd like some coffee and a sweet roll and I'll have the same," J. D. said.

Bennett sat at a great round table placed in a section of the kitchen J. D. referred to as the breakfast nook. Included in the area was a used brick fireplace, several gingham-covered club chairs, and ten maple captain's chairs that encircled a great Arthurian table. J. D.

140

chose a seat close to paned windows that looked out at the back garden, where chrysanthemums bloomed, bursts of oranges and yellows and whites against the green lawn.

"How's Polly?" J. D. asked Bennett.

"She's okay, J. D.," Bennett said.

"Well," J. D. said, leaning back in his chair, "to what do I owe this here honor?"

"Just happened to have a couple of minutes and thought I'd drop by."

"Uh-huh. Tell me, you working on that case downtown? Where those poor lost souls got slashed?"

"Yep."

"That what brings you up here where the rich folks live?"

"Yep."

"Uh-huh. Unusual, ain't it? The case taking you from there to here?"

Bennett had learned over the years to perk up and pay attention when J. D. began saying "ain't."

"Well, yes. It's unusual."

Elizabeth brought sweet rolls and coffee to the table and set everything down.

"You're looking pretty good," she told Bennett.

"Well, thanks, Elizabeth."

J. D. waited until she'd returned to her work outside the kitchen before speaking. "Trouble?" he asked quietly.

"I don't know. I don't think so."

"Uh-huh."

"Reason I came by is I was in the neighborhood. But, well, yes, something's come up that might get to be trouble."

J. D. bit a hunk out of his sweet roll, chewed and swallowed it, then sipped at his coffee.

"Do you think there's anything I could do to earn a living besides what I'm doing now?" Bennett asked.

"Well, I don't know. What's your opinion?"

"I'm not sure I have one. It's like Polly said, police work's all I've ever done. Besides being in Vietnam."

"What's Polly think?" J. D. asked. "She think you might be suited for something else?"

Bennett turned the coffee cup so the handle was closer to his right hand, then regarded it as if it held a secret. "She thinks I've never given anything else a try. She's right, of course. I haven't. But it'd be damn hard to spend a year thinking about other careers or jobs or whatever you want to call them, and that's what she's suggesting." He heard what he'd said, and suspected what J. D. was likely to do. "I'm not asking you for money," he said quickly.

"I know you're not."

"Anyway, that's what we've been discussing."

J. D. leaned forward, crossed arms on the table, "Your work scare Polly?" he asked.

Bennett nodded.

"I can't blame her," J. D. said. "When I asked you just now were you working on that case where those men've been slashed, and you said yes you were, why that scared me. My stomach just went straight down."

"Any job's dangerous, for Chrissake," Bennett said.

"Well, not any job," J. D. corrected. "I can name you jobs that there's no way can be described as dangerous, especially as compared to what you're up to."

Bennett didn't reply. He shrugged angrily.

"I can understand Polly's feelings," J. D. continued. "That's what I'm trying to point out to you. And I think she's got a good argument about you trying something else, testing adjoining waters, so to speak.

Hell, you got out of that Vietnam place and next thing anyone knows you're at the Police Academy."

"I like what I'm doing," Bennett stubbornly insisted. "I like it fine."

"Even if it costs you your wife?" J. D. asked. "Let's just suppose for a minute, here, that there was a compromise position to all this."

Bennett looked up from his coffee cup.

"If you was to take a leave of absence, look around, think about things, you and Polly, like she's suggesting, why, what's the harm in it?"

Bennett looked as though he was about to object. J. D. raised a heavy hand to stop him.

"I'd stake you," he said. "No questions. An investment on my part."

"I couldn't let you do that," Bennett said.

J. D. got steely. "You know about money talk," he said crisply. "Money talk is what I don't get into. I'll stake you, no questions from either party. It's a cheap way to find out if you're doing what's right for you and it's a cheap way to keep a marriage healthy. No more money talk, now."

Bennett knew better than to argue. He knew J. D. had money to spare, he'd learned over the years not to discuss where it came from or where it went. He suspected a combination of things, gambling for big stakes, shrewd investments in oil lands, never anything illegal, he was certain, but surely a wise old owl like J. D. pressed every opportunity to the limit.

So the matter was settled. Bennett didn't ask how much money was in the stake, or whether he was to ask for it as he needed it. In money matters, you left J. D. Cowper on his own.

They finished their coffee and talked about J. D.'s other children and how they were getting along in school, and J. D. bragged about them as he'd bragged about Bennett during his growing-up years. Then Bennett realized he'd have to move on or he'd miss his appointment with Franny Harris. J. D. walked him to his car, and Bennett drove back down the hill, out through the south Arluria gate and along the eastern edge of Bel Air, down Beverly Glen past Wilshire, until he found Berwin, a small, narrow street of well-maintained older homes.

He parked in front of 2023, a small white cottage with a roof overhang that provided shade in the summer and allowed the sun to enter wide front windows in the winter. The walk from street to front door was lined with zinnias, fall colors of earth tones, browns and dark yellows and oranges. The lawn was without weeds, so perfectly trimmed it seemed false. On the right side of the house a cement driveway ran from the street to a wooden garage at the rear of the property. The garage door was closed. Bennett walked to the front door and rang the bell. On the small porch were two old rocking chairs, painted beige, with a matching table between them.

When there was no answer to his ring, he rapped lightly on the door with his knuckles. Through the window to his right, he saw a dining room, furnished with a heavy round table, chairs, and sideboard, all of oak polished over the years to a deep gold. Through the other window, the one to his left, Bennett could see a living room, this also furnished with matching pieces, sofa, twin club chairs, two side chairs, side tables with reading lamps on them, and a low coffee table placed in front of the sofa. The upholstered furniture was covered in a bright floral pattern. This room, like the dining room, was immaculate. Aside from a few personal

144

items scattered about, knick-knacks and a magazine or two, the house might have been ready for rental.

Since no one had answered the door, Bennett wondered if Franny Harris had begun searching in the garage for the porcelain masks. He walked along the cement driveway to the back of the house. Here, also, was a lawn remarkably free of weeds. Two lemon trees and one orange filled the remainder of the small yard, which was bounded by a wooden fence, painted white to match the house, before which grew well-established poinsettias. The garage, doors closed, was also painted white. Attached to the garden side was a small lathhouse in which several pots, ready for filling, rested on a wood-slat counter. Franny Harris wasn't in her garden. Bennett walked to the back door and rang the bell. Through the windows on either side of the door he saw an enclosed back porch where a washing machine, dryer, and large food freezer were kept. Beyond, through an open doorway, he could see the kitchen, brightly papered in a floral pattern. He carefully tried the back door, but it was locked.

"Miss Harris?" he called. "Are you home?"

He was answered by a neighborhood dog, which began to bark excitedly. He walked over to the garage. The double doors were shut and locked and a chain was entwined between the door handles and held in place by a padlock.

"You looking for Ms. Harris?" a woman called.

A very pretty woman in jogging clothes was standing on the other side of the fence, on the property to the south of Bennett.

"Yes," he said. "I was supposed to meet her."

"I think she's gone out," the woman said. "About ten or fifteen minutes ago."

"Do you know when she's coming back?" Bennett

145

asked, walking over to the fence. He judged the woman to be in her mid-thirties. She had short, well-trimmed auburn hair and wore no makeup. Her skin radiated good health, although the beginning edges of crow's feet could be seen at the corners of her eyes.

"I have no idea," the woman said. "I was coming back from my morning run, and a man came by to pick her up." Then, trying to be agreeable, she said, "Maybe she's gone on an errand. One thing's for sure, if Ms. Harris says she has an appointment with you, she'll be there. Ms. Harris is a lady you can count on. The pride of the neighborhood. Den mother, you might say."

Bennett detected sarcasm in the words. "The man who picked her up," he said. "Does he live here with her?"

The woman laughed. "With Ms. Harris? God, no. I told you she's the neighborhood den mother. If one of us had a live-in man we weren't married to, we'd have to brave Ms. Harris's looks of scorn." She examined Bennett carefully. "You'll excuse me for speaking this way," she said. "I'm really very fond of Franny, and I suppose you're her best friend, or the husband of her best friend, and here I am being catty. It's not like me. Honest to God. I'm normally a regular respectful decent friendly soul who doesn't speak ill of anybody." She seemed honestly disturbed. "It's just that a while ago Ms. Harris got chummy with a male friend of mine, and told this nice gentleman about another male friend of mine, from whom I was not yet disengaged. I don't know if she did it to be mean, or if she's stupid and wasn't really aware of what she was doing and I suppose until I find out it would be wise of me to keep my big mouth shut. So." She shut her mouth firmly. It wasn't a big mouth, it was a normal-sized, well-shaped mouth. Then she laughed, showing such perfect teeth Bennett knew she'd worn braces as a child. "You'd like to know if she's coming back to meet you," the woman said. "The answer is I don't know because I don't know where she went. The reason I don't know where she went is I'm also something of a snooper, and when I'm at home during the day waiting for my agent to call and tell me I have a job or an interview, which is more likely, why then I look out my window from time to time to see what my neighbors are up to. Which gets us back to my answer to your question. I don't know where Ms. Harris went because I didn't recognize either her escort or his car. Absolute new pattern for Ms. Harris."

"When did they leave?" Bennett asked.

"As I told you, I think it was ten or fifteen minutes ago."

"And you'd never seen the man before? The one she was with?" Bennett asked.

She shook her head that she hadn't. "He's not easy to forget," she said. "I mean, there he was, carrying this box, a big box, and it looked heavy, and Ms. Harris wasn't helping him at all. He was struggling, I want to tell you."

"Why should she have been helping him?" Bennett asked, puzzled.

"Haven't you ever met Ms. Harris?" the woman asked, surprised.

"No," Bennett said. "I've never seen her in my life."

"Well, let's see, I'm five-six," the woman said, crinkling her eyes as she measured things in her head, "so Ms. Harris is about five-ten or -eleven in her stocking feet. Tall, handsome woman, snow white hair, face like an Indian princess, very regal, strong. And there she was striding along beside this man who was struggling

147

with this big heavy cardboard box—I can't imagine what was in it—and when they reached the car she just got in the front seat, the passenger side, and let this man open the trunk of his car and heft this box into the trunk. He couldn't get the lid closed. He found a length of rope in the trunk and tied the lid down as far as it would go. Then he hopped in and they drove away. I want to tell you, they were a picture."

Bennett still didn't understand. "Why a picture?" he wanted to know.

"Well," she explained, "I've told you about Ms. Harris, physically, I mean, what she looks like. Well there she was walking alongside this man who was carrying this big box and he's a little fellow, a little wiry man all dressed in black, black shoes, black slacks, a black watch-cap—isn't that what they call those knitted stocking caps sailors wear?"

Bennett said it was, as far as he knew. "This man," Bennett said. "You say you'd never seen him before?"

"Never. And believe me, a little fellow dressed like that. . . . If you'd seen him before you'd never forget him."

Bennett had to agree that was so. Once that little man dressed all in black got close to you, you weren't likely ever to forget him.

12

Bennett waited in his car. It was nearly noon when he saw Franny Harris walking down the street from a bus stop at the Beverly Glen corner. She was exactly as she'd been described, a tall, regal woman with snow white hair and the looks and manner of a princess. Bennett stepped out of his car and waited to greet her, a smile on his face. Peripherally, he was aware of the neighbor woman watching through the drawn curtains in her living room. She'd offered Bennett a drink or a cup of coffee while he waited for Franny Harris, but he'd declined.

"Good morning," he said to Franny Harris as she reached him. "My name's Fred Bennett."

"Oh yes," she said. "Charlie Oliver said you'd be by this morning. Come in, won't you?"

There was no apology for not having been there, no explanation. She was an unusually cool person. Bennett followed her up the walk to her front door, which she opened with a key taken from her purse, and into the house.

"Please sit down," she said, gesturing toward the living room Bennett had seen through the front window. He sat in one of the upholstered chairs. "Are you the man about the porcelain masks?" she asked, slipping out of her coat and hanging it in a closet off the entry.

"Yes, ma'am," he said, feeling like a schoolboy as she walked into the room and stood above him, towered above him, looking at him coldly.

"Well, I'm afraid I have bad news for you," she said. "I would have called if I'd known where to locate you. I no longer have those masks. And although I'm a fairly well-organized and structured person, as Charlie probably told you, I can't seem to find a record of what happened to them."

"Oh, that's too bad," Bennett said. "I'd wanted to take one back to Chicago with me. Haven't you any idea where they might be?" He looked up at her, trying to be as pleasant and ingenuous as he could. With his hard black eyes it was difficult.

"I have no idea where the masks are," she said softly. "None whatsoever. They could be on the moon at this instant, for all I know."

She stood there, waiting for him to leave.

"Charlie Oliver said they might be packed up in your garage," he said. "I'd be happy to help you move things around, if you'd like to take a look. Exercise would do me good."

"They're not in the garage," she said.

"Maybe stuck under something," Bennett suggested. "You know how things get stuck away."

"No, I don't know how things get stuck away," she said.

He smiled at her. "Well," he said, "I guess I'm out of luck."

"I guess you are." She hadn't moved. She stood above him, staring down. He tried to picture what she must have looked like striding along beside Sonny, while the little man struggled with a box that, Bennett was now convinced, held the remaining porcelain masks.

Bennett rose. "I'll leave you a number here in town where I can be reached," he said. "They're family, and I'm staying with them." He'd taken a notepad out of his pocket and a pen, and as he talked he wrote down his name and his home phone number. "I was going to stay at a hotel, but they wouldn't hear of it. When I told them I was coming out here to check out some things on the picture, they insisted I stay with them. Nice people," he concluded. "Cousins of my wife's." He handed Franny Harris the paper with his name and phone number on it. "You just call me there if you recollect where those masks might be. It's happened to me a million times, I lose track of something, think it's gone for good, and then all of a sudden in the middle of the night or when I'm occupied with a matter that's completely unrelated, it pops into my head where I left the thing I'd thought I'd lost or misplaced. So if it pops into your head where those masks might be, I'd certainly appreciate it if you'd give me a call at that number, they'll know where to reach me. Would you do that?" he asked her.

"Well, yes, I suppose I could," she said without committing herself.

"I certainly thank you for your time," Bennett said as he walked to the door. "I appreciate your kindness, having me into your house." He knew he wasn't overdoing it because she nearly smiled at **him** as she opened the door.

"Quite all right," she said.

"Well, I certainly hope I'll be hearing from you," he said.

She did smile, finally; an easy smile, one that could

have been interpreted as a smile of satsifaction. "Yes," she said enigmatically, and shut the door.

Bennett walked back to his car and left the neighborhood. He stopped at the first gas station and used the phone. He was able to reach Drang and arranged to meet him at a midway point, a hamburger place near the Miracle Mile area of the city.

Drang was already there, sitting in a booth in the rear of the restaurant, when Bennett arrived. The restaurant was decorated in Tudor English style, with burgundy leather banquettes along the walls and heavy wooden tables in the areas between. Drang was stirring a mug of coffee into which he'd just put sugar and cream.

"What's this about?" he asked Bennett, who slid in opposite him. "I just saw you a couple of hours ago."

"Very complex," Bennett answered, looking for a waiter.

"I was on my way out when you called," Drang said. "There's information on Sonny."

A waitress appeared, a middle-aged black woman in a starched uniform. "Get you something from the bar?" she asked.

"Coffee, please," Bennett said as she handed menus to the two men. As he looked at his menu, he said, "What information?"

"You're chasing a dead man," Drang said. "We've received a response to our A.P.B. this morning—a lucky response, to come that quickly—from someone who knew him in La Jolla. One of the officers on duty there this morning saw the A.P.B. the minute it came in and phoned. I want to save you some time, he told us. L. George Galley is no longer with us."

"When'd he die?" Bennett asked.

"That's what we're trying to find out," Drang said.

"We're not even sure it's the same Galley you're after. We don't know how old the man was or anything else about him."

The waitress came by to take their orders. Bennett had a hamburger with everything on it, and Drang had fruit salad.

"Do you know anything about the Gwen Thompson murder?" Bennett asked after the waitress had gone.

"No, I don't think so."

"She was Mrs. Salvatore Thompson. According to her father she was murdered a year and a half, two years ago. The case is unsolved, he says."

"Who's her father?" Drang asked.

Bennett told him about Charlie Oliver.

Drang stood up. "Be right back," he said.

He returned in five minutes, looking puzzled, and slid into the booth at the moment the waitress arrived with their meal. He waited until she had gone before speaking.

"According to our records," he said, "Mrs. Salvatore Thompson was a suicide."

Bennett began unscrewing the top of the catsup bottle.

"There was a question, for a while, as to whether it might have been murder. There was even a suspect. But the department decided, after the coroner had gone over the case thoroughly, that the woman had taken her own life."

"Who was the suspect?" Bennett asked.

"The dead man in La Jolla," Drang said. "L. George Galley."

Bennett poured catsup on his hamburger, which was already covered with cheese, lettuce, pickles and bacon. "I'll be a sonofabitch," he said. He bit into his sandwich, chewed carefully, and swallowed. "They're

153

sure they're talking about the L. George Galley in La Jolla? The recently dead man?"

"They're sure."

"Son-of-a-bitch," Bennett said once more.

They ate quietly. When they had finished, Bennett said, "I've got a lot of matters to attend to."

"So have I," Drang said.

Drang drove off without saying where he was going. Bennett headed back to Paramount. As a fan of late-night movies, he had thought that over the years the bad picture hadn't been made that he had not seen at least once. Yet he had no memory of ever having watched "The Dungeons of Hell County." He drove up to the studio entrance, giving a friendly salute to the same guard who'd been on duty earlier in the day. The guard frowned, then, like a teacher who wants a fractious class to know that fooling around is okay, but only up to a point; he waved Bennett through.

Bennett parked where he had before, and then hurried across the lot to the prop department. He opened the door and saw Lew Miller placing rifles in packing cases. Miller turned when he heard the door.

"Hey there," he greeted Bennett. "How you doin'?"

"Pretty good, pretty good," Bennett said, "if you can accept the fact that those porcelain masks have disappeared from sight."

"No kidding?" Miller said. "Charlie Oliver didn't have them? You saw him, didn't you?"

"Oh yeah, I saw him. He'd stored them somewhere, he told me his ex-secretary would know where."

"Franny Harris? Did you see Franny?"

"Oh yeah. She had no recollection of what happened to them."

"Franny doesn't remember? Impossible," Lew Miller said. "Franny Harris is a gal with a mind like a steel

154

trap. You drop a piece of information into Franny Harris's mind and plap!" he made a swift shutting sound, "it's there forever. Computers could take lessons from Franny Harris."

"Well, the exception's what makes the rule, I guess." Bennett commented, "because she doesn't know where the masks are or how they happened to disappear."

"Like you said, it's the exception that makes the rule." Lew Miller laid another rifle in the packing case he was filling. "Got to pack these things and get them loaded in the prop truck," he said. "Used to be you could find locations out in the San Fernando Valley. Now there's nothing to shoot but houses and department stores and factories and all that crap, and there's not even a place to put a camera, so we got to go up north, around Stockton, which is a long haul."

"I wonder if you could do me a favor," Bennett said.

"Sure, I can try. What's on your mind?"

"I'd like to see 'Dungeons' again. Maybe there's a way I could fake those masks for my picture. I can't really tell until I see the picture again."

"Oh, yeah," Lew Miller said. "I see what you mean. Well the place you want to go to do that is the distributor. There wouldn't be a print here on the lot. Whoever bought the distribution rights, he'd have a print you could see."

"Any idea who that could be?" Bennett asked.

"If you've got a minute I'll see if I can find out," Miller said.

Bennett said he had a minute, and sat in an empty chair. Lew Miller got behind his desk and opened his well-thumbed phone book. He found what he wanted, picked up the phone, and dialed an in-house number.

"Larry? Lew Miller. Listen," he said into the phone. "You remember a piece of crap we made in the olden days called 'The Dungeons of Hell County'? That's the one. Oh, yeah, awful, really awful. Listen—a friend of mine has a reason to see it, do you know who the distributor is?" He listened, then roared with laughter. "That's really funny," he said to Bennett. "He wants to know is my friend paying off a bet or doing penance." He spoke into the phone again. "That's funny," he said to Larry. "My friend cracked up." He listened again, reaching for a pencil buried under the piles of papers on his desk. "Yeah. You sure? No, I'll call him. Thanks, Larry." He hung up. "He thinks he knows who might know," he told Bennett. "Let's try it."

This time he dialed a number off the lot. "Samuel Bellows," he told whoever had answered the phone. "Tell him it's Lew Miller at Paramount." While he waited for the connection he said to Bennett, "I think he'll remember me. He was in the production department here. . . . Sam? Lew Miller. How are you?" he said into the phone. "Couldn't be better," he said. "For an old fart I do pretty good. Get my share, you know me. Listen Sam, I won't keep you. This friend of mine has a reason why he has to see a piece of crap we made here years ago, 'The Dungeons of Hell County'; I hear you guys are distributing it to television and anyone else stupid enough to pay good money. That's the one. L. George's picture." He listened. "I don't know what the hell happened to him. I heard he was dead. Yeah. Nice guy. Yeah, I'll wait." He put his hand over the mouthpiece. "He's the distributor," he confirmed. "He's checking to see if he's got a print there, or if all of them are out. Yeah, Sam, I'm here." He listened. "Marvelous. Could my friend . . . marvelous." He picked up his pencil once again, and wrote as he listened. "Got it," he said. "I'll ask him." Then, to

156

Bennett: "When could you see it? He's got a print there. He says it's scratchy if you don't mind."

"I don't mind," Bennett said. "Sooner the better."

Lew Miller spoke into the phone again. "The sooner the better," he said, "and he digs scratchy. He says to tell you where he comes from in Chicago, scratchy is all he sees." He listened, and then laughed again. "He'll be there. Listen, Samuel, I appreciate. I owe you one. Right." He hung up and handed Bennett a piece of paper on which he'd written an address. "Sam says right now, if you want. I wrote his name, and the company name, and the address. Now let's see, you know where Romaine is? Romaine's between Santa Monica and Melrose. Closer to Santa Monica. They're in a building this side of La Brea. He said park across the street and they'll validate it. That take care of it for you?"

Bennett took the paper and stood. "Oh yeah," he said. "Listen, speaking of owing somebody one, I owe you a dozen."

Lew Miller waved it off. "Just tell Pinky," he said. "I'm glad I could be of some help. But I'd appreciate it if you'd let Pinky know, because I did owe him some from a couple years ago."

Bennett found the Romaine address without any trouble. He parked across the street, left his keys in the car as a surly old man told him to, and entered an ancient building with a modern front, the main office of the modestly named Great Films Incorporated. The receptionist sat behind a half-wall of glass, in an enclosed area only large enough to contain her and her desk and chair. The glass had a round hole in it, and Bennett leaned forward and delivered his name into it. The receptionist fumbled at some papers on her desk, discov-

157

ered what she was looking for, and slid it to Bennett through a chute at the bottom of her half-glass cage.

"Projection Room 4," she said, sounding as though she might fall asleep before she finished speaking. "Through the door, right, then left."

She pressed a hidden button, and as Bennett picked up his studio pass a buzzer released the lock at the entry door. Bennett smiled his thanks and entered the main section of the building. He turned right and walked down a sagging and creaking corridor, then turned left. Before him was a heavier door, on which was printed Projection Room 4. He entered a very untheater-like room in which half a dozen folding chairs faced a small screen. Behind Bennett, on the wall opposite the screen, was the projection porthole. The projectionist must have been waiting, for as soon as Bennett entered the room the lights went out. He sat on the chair nearest him as the projector began unspooling a sixteen-millimeter print, more like a home movie then a theatrical film. The academy leader numbers flashed on the screen, a countdown from ten, until, where zero would have been, the picture began. Garish theme music, scratchy and with the pitch wowing with age, backed the studio credits and main title.

Lew Miller had called the picture a piece of crap. He'd also said it was awful, dreadful. In Bennett's view Lew Miller was being kind. The setting was a small town in New England, somewhere in Maine or Vermont or New Hampshire, although, inexplicably, whenever the camera moved one way or the other, palm trees could be seen behind the actors. Hell County, it turned out, was so named because all the people who lived there had basements in their homes, and the basements were fitted out as torture chambers, with

158

iron maidens and thumbscrews and machinery for drawing and quartering, and whips and chains and iron-studded harnesses. It was not clear whether the torture was administered to strangers who wandered unknowingly into this vile community, or whether the natives did it to each other while having fun and games. Every now and then, for no reason that Bennett could at first fathom, people were disguised in porcelain masks. The effect was startling. It was as if a beauty shop had opened in a manure pile. Both men and women wore the masks, or so it would seem if the yardstick was the actors' wardrobe, and if you assumed that dresses were costumes for women and trousers for men.

There was no story that Bennett could follow, except that evil lurked in the hearts of the men and women who lived in the strange place where unmeltable snow and dusty palm trees coexisted. After seeing the masks in small groupings two or three times during the picture, (including three department-store sequences), Bennett was able to count them in the climactic scene, where the townspeople gathered to worship their Devil God for the last time before the big fire, which had been set by someone who wanted to get even because of past terrible things that had been done, burned everything to the ground. There were sixteen masks in that scene. Bennett figured that must have been all the masks at hand, all that had not been broken or lost, because if more of them had been available they would have been used. He had been able to identify only four different actors in the picture. The masks, he guessed, were used by the actors when they were playing someone else. In the climactic scene, where sixteen people appeared, everyone on the set must have donned a mask and stepped before the camera. The masks accomplished two things: they made it impossible to know whether you were looking at a man or a woman (only the wardrobe gave a clue), and they were so outrageous when worn that they shocked you into not paying attention to anything else that was happening.

The picture finally, humanely, was over, and the lights came up. Bennett stood, waved thank you toward the projection booth, and walked out. He had his parking ticket validated by the receptionist, who wouldn't do it until he gave her back the studio pass she'd handed him when he'd entered the building. He retrieved his car, which by then was buried behind three other vehicles, all of which had to be moved by the surly old man who acted as though it was Bennett who had the responsibility for organizing the comings and goings at that parking lot, and had screwed up, somehow.

The picture had been awful, but one thing stuck. When you saw someone wearing a porcelain mask, you didn't watch anything else. The outrageous mask caught and held your complete attention. It was not something you would ever forget or mistake for anything else. And if the mask wearer wore only black, there was absolutely no way of making any identification, except for the general size of the individual. Sonny, for example. Small, wiry, strong.

Like the man who'd been seen carrying the cardboard box from Franny Harris's house or garage.

Or who looked like L. George Galley, as Lew Miller had described him. Small, wiry, strong. The way he looked in the publicity picture. A man who was reported to be dead. No longer with us, the La Jolla cop had said.

Bennett drove back to Charlie Oliver's house on Corsicana in Bel Air. He pulled into the curved drive

160

She turned to him, her face sad and tired. "It's not you. It's me. I can't compete, and I feel like I'm supposed to, I feel as though to be a good wife I should take a back seat and leave the driving to you and be grateful for whatever crumbs come my way." She touched her forehead with a wet hand, held the hand there, as though trying to cool off her thoughts. "Do you think I'm spoiled?" she asked.

The question caught him off guard. "Why'd you ask that?" he wanted to know.

"My mother always told me I was spoiled. She said my dad spoiled me rotten. She said that anything I wanted I got because my dad couldn't say no to me. Do you think that's true?"

"No, of course not," Bennett said. "I think right now we're having a rough time because we have to deal with this job I have, but I don't think you're spoiled. I think you're a hell of a person."

"Do you?" she asked him.

"Oh, God yes," he said, his voice shaking. "I'd like to be able to tell you how much you really mean to me but I can't. I haven't got the words. Then it seems like every time I try to show you I get caught up in that damn job."

She started to speak but he put his fingers over her mouth.

"You know what we've been talking about? About having options? Time to look around? Well, maybe it can be done. When I get this case out of the way, we'll talk about it. There's a way it might be done." He didn't tell her that J. D. had offered the money because he wasn't sure she'd accept the idea. She liked her father-in-law but didn't understand him and hadn't ever been able to get close to him because she felt that J. D.

gave priority to Bennett's needs, not hers. "Can you hang on?" Bennett asked.

She stood there, coolly elegant, blonde hair tied back, wearing no makeup, dressed in an ancient terry shirt and ragged jeans, looking like a young Grace Kelly. "I think so," she said. "I want to, and that's half the battle, isn't it?"

He agreed it was.

He showered and changed his clothes and was packing his bag when the phone rang. Polly answered it in the kitchen.

"It's Rufus," she called.

Bennett picked up the bedroom phone.

"Another body," Drang said.

"Same killer?" Bennett asked.

"Seems to be," Drang said. "Carbon copy of the other murders. Only one difference."

"What's that?"

"It wasn't found downtown, where the others were killed. This one was in West Hollywood."

"He's moving into the high-rent district," Bennett said. "I wonder where he's headed?"

13

Bennett drove south on the San Diego freeway. He ran into heavy traffic near Los Angeles airport, and again at the curve that swung past Long Beach and the interchanges with the Harbor and Long Beach freeways. He'd packed a small bag with a change of clothes in case he had to stay more than one night.

"You going to check in with the La Jolla police?" Drang had asked, when Bennett told him where he was headed.

Bennett had said he wasn't.

"Why go now?" Drang had asked. "Wait until morning. You can't accomplish anything at night."

Bennett had said that Drang sounded like Polly. He was going now, he had said, because if he waited until morning, he'd have wasted half a day.

"Beats hell out of me," Drang had said. "We've got a fresh unsolved murder in West Hollywood, and you're driving to La Jolla."

" 'Let every man mind his own business.' Cervantes, as if you didn't know," Bennett had said before he hung up.

He turned on the car radio to an all-news station and listened to the newsperson tell about Government plans to control inflation, cut taxes, solve crime, find energy sources, and restore the nation to a preeminent position in world affairs. Not mentioned was how this was to be done. Then he listened to the sportscaster's views on what would be happening over the coming weekend in the violent world of football. Next a weatherman explained why he'd been wrong for the past few days, when he'd predicted an eighty percent chance of rain, heavy at times, when the reality of the matter was that it had become unusually warm because of a Santa Ana that had blown up because of a barometric high that had settled in over Nevada and Utah. The new forecast was warmer days, he avowed, and some wind. Local news followed, with crime leading the way, and the top story was about the newly found body of a man who'd been slashed to death in West Hollywood, which was unusual because similar crimes in the past month or so had all occurred in the seediest part of the city, on skid row, where bums and alcoholics hung out, and now a shabbily dressed man, still unidentified, had been found similarly murdered, but in a classier neighborhood where upper-middle-class people lived. The newscaster sounded affronted, as though murder in the downtown gone-to-seed part of the city was as acceptable as murder could be; but when it got out to the west side, why, that was another story, and it was time to do something about it.

Bennett found a music station broadcasting a recorded jazz concert and drove to the strains of Ellington and Basie and Miles Davis and Oscar Peterson. He made the La Jolla turnoff at about seven, and decided to look for Charlie Oliver's house before settling on a place to stay for the night. He stopped at the first open gas station he saw, filled his tank and got directions on how to find Avenida Rojo.

166

The freeway had been cut high on the hill, and Bennett swung down toward the sea on gently curving roads to reach the Oliver house. He located Avenida Rojo and followed it to the beach. There it made a right turn and continued parallel to the sand, a community of rich comfortable homes whose inhabitants enjoyed one of the best of all worlds, in Bennett's view: they owned a piece of land that gave them private access to the Pacific Ocean. He remembered the housekeeper's description, and there, at the corner of the ocean, as she had put it, where the street followed the line of the beach and made a sharp turn, was a large, comfortable Spanish house, white stucco with a red tiled roof, built in a U shape around a courtyard. Every room was lighted, and Bennett could see Eileen, Charlie Oliver's granddaughter, sitting in the living room watching television. He parked and went to the door. After a moment, Eileen opened it. She stared up at him for a second, then grinned broadly.

"Hey, hello," she said. "What're you doing down here?"

"I found out something I thought your granddad should know, and I had to drive to La Jolla anyway. . . ."

"Who is it?" Charlie Oliver yelled from another part of the house.

"It's the man you were talking to this morning," Eileen called. "Mr. Bennett."

Charlie Oliver appeared from the beach side of the house, wearing sandals, swimming trunks, and another Hawaiian shirt, this one depicting a field of pineapples tended by beautiful young women who were attempting to harvest the fruit while dancing the hula.

"Well for goodness sakes," Charlie Oliver said. "How'd you find us?"

167

Bennett said the housekeeper had told him where they were. "I had to come down anyhow," he said, "so I thought I'd stop by. I have some information that might interest you."

"Well come on in," Oliver said, tanned bandy legs quickly moving as he scuttled back into the room. "Let's have a cocktail."

"Grandpa," Eileen said warningly.

"You go watch television," her grandfather told her. "When I say cocktail I mean a very light drink. Not enough alcohol to wet a gnat."

"And only one," she warned, as she went back into the living room.

Bennett followed Oliver into a taproom on the ocean side of the house, a room with glass doors opening onto a used-brick patio that adjoined the wide beach. A low brick wall separated the patio from the sand. The room was paneled with dark wood and the floor was covered with large, deep-red tiles burnished by polish and wear. A pub-like bar filled the wall opposite the glass doors, one small section of the counter hinged open. Oliver slid through the opening.

"What'll you have?" he asked. An old-fashioned glass was already on the bar top. In it, besides a dark liquid, were a maraschino cherry and a slice of orange.

"Scotch," Bennett said. "On the rocks."

Oliver grabbed a glass from the back bar, dumped a couple of ice cubes in it, and filled it with Scotch from a bottle under the counter. He slid the drink to Bennett.

"Here you go," he said. "Cheers." He raised his glass, Bennett his, and they drank.

"What information?" Oliver asked.

"About your daughter," Bennett said.

The old man's face tightened.

168

"I'm not prying," Bennett quickly assured him. "But I know a guy on the L.A.P.D., a captain of detectives, and I was talking to him about something else entirely, and your name came up, and what had happened to your daughter, and I told him what you'd said, that it was unsolved, and you know what my friend told me?"

Charlie Oliver stared into his glass.

"My friend on the L.A.P.D. told me the only suspect they had is dead."

Charlie Oliver nodded. Bennett wasn't sure whether it was an acknowledgment of news, or an admission that Oliver already had that information.

"My friend told me this man's name," Bennett continued. Charlie Oliver looked up from his glass.

"L. George Galley," he said in a whisper.

"Yeah. Right," Bennett said. "L. George Galley. Isn't he the fella who made that picture where they used those masks I wanted to get my hands on?"

"The very same."

"He's dead, my friend on the L.A.P.D. told me."

"So I heard." Spoken in a dry brittle voice.

"My friend told me this L. George Galley lived down here in La Jolla. Did you know him?"

"I met him."

"That's all? You met him?"

Charlie Oliver's hand shook when he tried to pick up his glass. He used both hands, holding the glass like a chalice, bringing it slowly to his lips, then gulping a mouthful of liquid.

"I know this is none of my business," Bennett said, "but this guy on the L.A.P.D., his name's Drang, Rufus is his first name; I've known him for a couple of years, and well, you know how it is, you hear something startling, like what you said to me this morning about your daughter, and I just couldn't keep my mouth shut when I was with him, I just kind of blurted it out about what had happened to your daughter, and how you'd said the case was unsolved, and that's when I got the information I just passed on to you. Did you already know about it? That L. George Galley was a suspect? Is that his name, L. George Galley?"

"I knew about it. And you're not prying. It's very decent of you to show an interest."

The old man looked beaten, Bennett thought, as if the revived memory of what had happened to his daughter was physical punishment. He leaned on the bar as though he had a sudden bellyache, his face pale, his head down.

"Are you all right?" Bennett asked.

Charlie Oliver nodded. After a moment, he said, "He seduced her."

"L. George Galley?"

"He seduced my daughter. She was married, had a beautiful baby girl, Eileen wasn't a baby really, when it happened; but he seduced my daughter. It was a bad time. A terrible time. She was a good girl, she'd never gotten into any trouble. Sal, her husband? I think he was probably the first man she'd ever known, known intimately. She dated, she went out with boys, petted, necked, whatever they call it now, but I believe Sal, her husband, was the first man she'd ever known. And then she got mixed up with L. George Galley, that lousy arrogant little prick, that deceitful, lying bastard, and he seduced her. He seduced Gwen."

"Did her husband know about it?" Bennett asked.

"I don't know," Charlie Oliver said. "I figured, why make matters worse by asking a lot of questions. I kept my mouth shut. Shut tight. I didn't ask and I didn't tell. No questions, and no judgments."

"Where did L. George live?" Bennett asked.

"On this same beach," Oliver said bitterly. "Just north of here, around the bend on this same beach. Gwen was spending the summer here, in this house, when it happened. She had the baby here with her. Sal was working in town and he'd come down weekends. I let them have full use of this house, and that's when it happened."

The painful memory brought tears to his eyes. "That arrogant little prick," he repeated, his voice broken. "Why would a woman let a man like that get close to her?" He hadn't asked Bennett the question, it was addressed to the gods.

"Was Galley married?" Bennett asked.

"I think he was, a long time ago. That's what I heard, anyway. I don't know, except what I heard." He finished his drink then looked quickly to see if Eileen was in sight, and hastily poured some more whiskey into his old-fashioned glass. "It's all right," he assured Bennett. "Little Miss Worrywart makes a federal case out of nothing."

Bennett emptied his glass, and Charlie Oliver grabbed it, added ice and Scotch, and pushed it back across the bar.

"There you go," he said.

Bennett thanked him, and swirled the ice with his index finger. "Your daughter met L. George Galley when Eileen was a child. How long ago?"

The old man thought about it. "Eileen was only two or three years old," he said.

"Did anything go on between your daughter and Galley after those first meetings?"

The old man didn't seem to understand.

"I know it's none of my business," Bennett apologized, "but they first met nine or ten years ago. What do you suppose happened that caused your daughter's

171

death? Had she and Galley continued seeing one another?" Charlie Oliver didn't reply. "When did Galley die?" Bennett asked. "Do you know?"

"Couple of weeks ago," Charlie Oliver said. "Or so I heard."

"It's strange, don't you think?"

The old man sipped his fresh drink. "Yes," he agreed. "It's strange, all right."

Eileen appeared at the door and saw the glass in front of her grandfather.

"What are you doing?" she yelled. "Can't I leave you alone for three seconds?" She ran to the bar and picked up the glass and held it to her nose. "Not enough booze to wet a gnat," she said, in a pretty good imitation of her grandfather's voice. She turned on Bennett. "And you were just going to sit there and watch him slowly kill himself," she accused. "Shame on you."

Bennett thought the wisest thing he could do was keep quiet.

"It's okay," Charlie Oliver said to the girl. "I haven't had enough to make any difference."

The expression on her face changed from anger to such love and understanding that Bennett's heart melted.

"You go along," Charlie Oliver told his granddaughter. "I give you my solemn word nothing's going to happen. Scout's honor," he said, holding up his right hand, pinky held down by the thumb. "Now go along."

She ran around the bar and Charlie Oliver met her at the opening. She hugged her grandfather and he kissed her, patted her tiny backside as she turned and left the room.

"She worries too damn much," the old man said, "and I don't know what to do about it. I suppose the

172

root of it is she thinks because her mother got killed and then her father went away, that I will too. She's too young to understand everybody has to go off with death sooner or later, and that doesn't mean she's being deserted." He gave an enormous sigh. "Hardly a fresh or original problem in the raising of the young," he said.

Bennett finished his drink and stood. "Well," he said, "I've got to move along."

"Thanks for coming by," Charlie Oliver said, walking him to the door. "Very decent of you."

"Had to be down here anyway," Bennett said. As the old man opened the door, Bennett said: "This Galley? Did you say he lived on the beach?"

"On Avenida Azul," Oliver said. "This is Rojo. Blanco is up on the hill. Clever land developer, to have thought of it. Three cheers."

"Anybody living in his house?" Bennett asked. "I wonder if maybe it's for sale."

"I have no idea," Charlie Oliver said. "I was so happy to hear the arrogant little bastard was dead I never asked any questions about the property. The number's 551, if you want to check it out. Big wooden house, weathered. Nice beach."

The old man waited at the door until Bennett drove away, then went back inside his house.

Bennett found a motel on Prospect Avenue, in a tourist section complete with shops and restaurants, and checked in. He bought some Scotch at a liquor store across the street, poured himself a drink, then sat on the bed to watch the evening news before going out for dinner. He tuned in just as the flash came on. The young man on camera held up a piece of paper someone had just handed him. "Big breaking story up in Los Angeles," he said. "Los Angeles Police Chief

173

Robinson Victor has just announced the arrest of the man alleged to have committed the recent slashing murders in that city. Police are withholding the name of the alleged killer in those crimes, but Chief Victor said the public can sleep tonight knowing no further murders of that sort will occur. We've got our man, Chief Victor said."

Bennett picked up the phone before the newscaster had finished. He gave the motel desk Drang's phone number in Los Angeles.

"Where are you?" Drang asked when the connection was made and Bennett identified himself.

"I told you, La Jolla," Bennett said. "What's this nonsense about arresting a killer? I just saw it on TV."

"Well, we've been investigating this case with you and without you," Drang explained carefully. "I told you I didn't know what you were going to be doing in La Jolla, when the crimes were being committed up here. The Chief has taken a personal interest in the case, and he's put together what you've come up with and what some of the other officers have come up with, and when an identification was made by officers working the downtown area and a man was picked up who answered the descriptions we have of the killer, that man was booked and he's now in custody."

"You've made a mistake," Bennett said.

"I don't think so," Drang said.

"You have. This is a hell of a lot more complicated than it seems to be," Bennett said. He was getting angry.

Drang's voice turned icy. "You get back here," he said. "We've got our man. No question about it."

"You haven't," Bennett said. "You're not even close."

"Get back here," Drang said.

"Up yours,". Bennett said. He was so furious by then that he slammed down the phone.

And if all the worst things of Frederick Bennett's future life had a starting place, if everything bad that was to happen to him needed a date and a time for the clock to start, the moment was then, in a motel room in La Jolla.

14

Bennett had little patience with people who jumped to conclusions, and less with the strivers for power who leap-frogged to their goal, overstepping reason, discussion, and well-thought-out procedures. He also had a temper. And one of the things that infuriated him most was the person who didn't hear him out.

Which explains how he felt that evening in the motel room in La Jolla. Not heard out. Surrounded by ambitious men who leap-frogged. Infuriated by these conditions. He probably could have saved the day by making a quick return phone call in which he said things like, "Sorry, Drang, I just got pissed off because I've been working so hard on this thing," the sort of explanation that Drang, because he knew Bennett so well, would have accepted.

But Bennett was dogged. Stubborn, would perhaps be a better word. And so he didn't call Drang. He sat there in his motel room and used all the cuss words he'd ever heard, in whatever language he'd ever heard them, and finished the drink he'd made himself. Then he left the room, and entered a small cafe next door to the motel, and ate the special of the day, which was freshly caught red snapper, prepared with onions and green peppers and tomatoes, and despite the furies the conversation with Drang had loosed, he ate all the food and almost enjoyed it.

After dinner he got back in his car and drove to the house L. George Galley had lived in, on Avenida Azul on the beach just north of Charlie Oliver's home. He didn't know what he'd find, or even what he'd do when he got there, but in the face of the news that a man in Los Angeles was under arrest on suspicion of the slashings, he felt compelled to continue his own course on the case.

The street was crowded with cars. Bennett parked a block away from the beach and walked back. A light fog lay on the water, muffling the surf's sound. L. George Galley's house was a great two-storied building of weathered boards, looking ancient and modern at the same time. Blinds and shutters on the street side of the house were drawn, but light leaked through slits, touching grass and the trees and thick bushes that encircled the property. From inside the house Bennett heard music playing, exotic drums and flutes punctuated by sudden strident voices. He walked to the front door, which was flanked by glass panels draped in a gauzy material that revealed moving shadows and figures, but made it impossible to identify what he was looking at. Someone inside the house had seen him coming or somehow was aware that he was standing there because the door was suddenly opened from the inside. Bennett blinked.

Facing him was a man or a woman, he wasn't able to tell which, dressed in loose-fitting cotton pants and brocade slippers turned up at the toes, a full long-sleeved blouse that buttoned high on the throat, and a tuban-like hat, all in various shades of red. Whoever the person was, he or she wore a porcelain mask ex-

177

actly the duplicate of the ones Bennett had been searching for.

"Yes?" this person said, in what could have been a male's reedy tenor or a female's husky contralto.

"Mr. Galley?" Bennett asked. It was the first thought that came to his mind.

"He is no longer with us," said the voice. The mask's pert mouth pouted like a lipstick advertisement.

In the room behind the costumed person who'd opened the door, Bennett was able to see other costumed people going from what seemed to be a bar, into what seemed to be a living room. Furniture was pushed aside, and floor spaces were crowded with enormous velvet pillows, on which other costumed figures lay singly or in combinations.

"Are you fuzz?" the voice asked, then giggled.

"What, me? Fuzz?" Bennett repeated in his best incredulous voice. "Is that a compliment or an insult?"

Another figure appeared behind the first one. This person wore a caftan and could have been a male Greek dancer or a female Moroccan hostess. The garment was striped in dark green over an off-white base. And a porcelain mask covered the face.

"What is it?" the second person asked in a voice that, again, might have been a high-register male or a deep-throated female.

"Well, as far as I can tell," said the first person, "it's a male."

"There's always room for one of them," the second person said.

"Is there another mask?" the first person asked.

"I'll see," the second person said, and withdrew toward the inner part of the house.

"Who knows," the first person said, "there might be

178

another mask, and if you put on one of them you're anything and everything."

"They're very attractive," Bennett said. "Where'd you get hold of them?"

"Oh you're getting into deep dark secrets," the first person said. "I'll bet you're the sort of person who'd kiss and tell, asking questions like that."

The second person reappeared, carrying a porcelain mask. "It's the last mask," this person said.

"Cole Porter wrote that," first person said. "It's the last mask, dah dah dah dum," and first person floated around the entrance room, loose-fitting pants billowing, turned up shoes creaking against the polished wood floor.

The second person handed Bennett a porcelain mask. "Did you say Mr. Galley was no longer with us?" Bennett asked as he accepted it.

"Gone but not forgotten," the first person said, the dance completed. "Nothing left but memories, which tonight we celebrate."

By then Bennett was certain he'd stumbled into the recreation wing of a mental hospital. From within the house, the sweet smell of marijuana drifted by. Directly in Bennett's line of vision stood two people, both masked, one dressed in white tie and tails, the other in a gown that might have been stolen from Ginger Rogers' wardrobe closet. They were touching each other—exploratory touching, hands running across bodies, examining. First person noticed what held Bennett's attention.

"Before you take off the mask, you have to find out what your partner is," first person explained. "That's our new game. The two persons you're watching? He's a her, and she's a him." This followed by the giggle Bennett had heard earlier. "When she finds his pecker and he finds her honey pot off come the masks and they disappear together. And if I may say so, it's a nicer way of meeting people than taking out an ad in your church paper."

"Or going from bar to bar," second person added. "Everyone you meet here is on the up-and-up."

"Up and up. Exactly," first person cracked up, giggle chased giggle. "Which is why this evening has been called a Galley Gala," squeezed through the giggle.

"Once you put on your mask no one will know if you're a girl or a boy," second person said.

"I'll know," first person said, and whirled in place, harem pants flapping in the breeze. When the turn was complete, first person's left hand darted out and quickly touched the front of Bennett's trousers. "That's the way to tell," first person said. "A little pat here and a little pat there."

"Is this the first time you've used these masks?" Bennett asked. He felt like a fool, standing there with a porcelain mask in his hand, talking to what he was convinced were insane people, but they had information he needed and he plunged ahead. "I mean, they're very unusual. Where'd you get them?"

"They're fairly new," first person said. Then, facing second person, "Wouldn't you say they're fairly new?"

"Very fairly," second person said.

"Oh good. Marvelous," first person giggled. Lamplight glinted on the porcelain, on the expressionless face, eyebrows coyly arched, turned-up nose perfectly shaped, red lips half-open invitingly, skin the color of a china doll. "Very fairly. What a marvelous answer."

"Thank you," second person said.

"Where were they before they were here?" Bennett asked.

"Ahhh, you see?" first person said. "The story tantalizes. Tantalus is the root of the word. What a devil that Tantalus was, tantalizing."

"Mr. Galley had them made for a movie," Bennett said. Then, in answer to both masks, which had quickly turned toward him: "He told me that, that he'd had them made. Later, after the movie had been released, he sold them, and they disappeared, probably stored in someone's garage." He wished he could see their faces, watch their eyes, so he could judge the reaction his story was getting, but two blank masks stared at him. It made him redefine deadpan. "Then they disappeared from the garage and here they are. I wonder who found them, and where they were found, and why they showed up here?"

First person leaned closer, as though Bennett had an odor which would further identify him. "Are you some kind of mask freak?" first person sniffed.

"Hell no," Bennett replied. "As far as I am personally concerned, I just came by here to say how do to Mr. Galley, and you folks told me he wasn't with us any longer, which I take to mean he's expired, gone to that great beach up in the sky . . ." he stopped to catch his breath, and it gave first person a chance to giggle, "and the two of you brought up this whole mask business, brought it up so stylishly it provoked my interest; and when my interest is provoked I ask questions, which brings us to where we are."

For a finish, he held the mask up before his face, and felt the touch of the cool dispassionate porcelain.

"Perfect," the first person said. "Isn't it perfect?"

Second person agreed enthusiastically. "Perfect! Just perfect!"

"Put the band around your head to keep it on," first

181

person said, "and circulate." First person's mask faced second person. "It's perfect," first person repeated.

Bennett was about to put on the mask when he saw two figures standing in a shadowy room on the beach side of the house. One of them was tall, the other short. He wasn't able to see what they wore, or whether they were men or women, but their sudden appearance in this room of so many masks made him think of Franny Harris and Sonny. He put on the mask that had been given him, feeling foolish as he did so. He had never been a cheerful game player: he wasn't a man who was able to spend his time on pure happiness, some grit had to be mixed with it. In this instance, as he placed the band that held the mask around his head, he decided this could be considered part of his job, even though the couple who had been examining one another were now quite openly caressing intimate portions of each other's body, a business better done in privacy, in Bennett's view.

First person reached up to adjust Bennett's mask, and the odor of delicate perfume rose from the red costume. "Wouldn't you like to know what I am?" first person whispered provocatively. "Touch and see."

Bennett pretended he hadn't heard, muttered thanks through the mask, hearing his own voice reflected back to him, and stepped into the center of the party. The room in which he had seen the tall-and-short couple opened onto a wooden deck. Only candles, burning in glass lanterns, their flickering flames throwing grotesque shadows, lighted the guests who were here. As Bennett's eyes became accustomed to the darkness, he was startled to see the activity around him close-up. Lines of cocaine had been placed in a flat glass dish, and directly before him a masked figure stuck a soda straw into a mask, and snorted a line of powder off the

182

plate. To his right, two unmasked bearded men made love, while just beyond them, two unmasked women fondled each other brazenly, legs widely open. He felt a hand touch his thigh, and a voice whispered something he couldn't hear. He saw a sudden movement on the outdoor deck and thought he recognized the Mutt and Jeff couple. He hurried through the room, his breathing difficult in the mask, which fitted his head and face closely.

Outside on the deck, a soft breeze blew in from the sea, touching the shore and stirring the thin fog layer Bennett had seen when he first arrived. The couple were gone. Bennett hurried to the edge of the deck. He thought he saw movement to the south, in the direction of Charlie Oliver's house, but it was a moonless night, and the moving shadows might have been thrown by the couple, or by the trees and bushes that grew alongside the rich homes that lined this strand.

Bennett stepped off the deck and began walking south in the soft sand. He removed the mask when he was away from the Galley house, holding it by the headband.

He was certain that Drang and Chief Victor were mistaken and had picked up the wrong man. He believed they had gone wrong out of their eagerness to solve the case, finish off the matter with one big media event where the chief could hold another of his famous press conferences, in which, facing banks of cameras and microphones, he would praise his talented, efficient organization, suggesting that only since he had come to power had the resource been properly used. Bennett wasn't fond of Chief Victor. He felt the chief was the least qualified man for the job in the upper echelons of the department. In fact, the chief had ranked sixth in the Civil Service examinations the top eight men in the department had taken. But when it became time for the Commission to choose a new chief, it was Robinson Victor who had been selected. Some people in town thought it was a political move, some suspected that Victor had a black book crammed with names and peccadilloes. These people felt that the chief didn't even have to use his book, or threaten to use it. It was known that he had it, and Robinson Victor was acknowledged to be a man with ambition so strong he wouldn't allow anything to stop his forward motion. So, for whatever combination of reasons, the new chief of the L.A.P.D. was Robinson Victor.

The first slashing murder occurred the day after he was sworn in, in the rattiest part of the downtown area. And Chief Victor had jumped on the case, held press conferences, promised immediate swift action (swift was one of his favorite words), and now he'd made an arrest, announced to the world that he'd gotten his man—and in Bennett's view they weren't even close.

But Bennett didn't have facts to back up his opinion. And if he did come up with another suspect, he would be in trouble within the department. The chief wasn't about to be tripped up by a plainclothes officer named Frederick Bennett. Not Robinson Victor. Not on your life.

And far back in his head Bennett knew that, and began to realize he had pushed himself between a rock and a hard place.

He'd almost reached Charlie Oliver's house. He could see the red-tile roof and the U-shaped building just ahead. The house was dark. Earlier, when Bennett had approached from the street side, every room had been lighted, and it had appeared to be a warm, friendly home. Now it seemed to Bennett there was something sinister about it. From this point of view on the beach, the hills behind it, which were foreshortened in the darkness, threatened to crowd the building into the sea. Bennett shook off his morbid feelings and continued walking, the soft sand muffling his steps. The placid surf was made up of small inconsequential rollers, the sort that might be found on a wind-protected inland lake. It was so quiet that between the plop of the rollers, Bennett could hear loose change jingling in his pants pocket. He was only a dozen feet from the house when he heard the scream. It was so unexpected, tore so abruptly into the night, that at first he wasn't able to identify it. The second scream was more piercing than the first. Bennett dropped the mask in the sand and ran toward the house, where lights were turning on with the speed of a chain of firecrackers. At the patio door, suddenly silhouetted by the interior light, stood two figures, one tall, the other short. They saw Bennett racing toward them, turned, and ran in the opposite direction, through the house and out the front door. Charlie Oliver rushed down the stairs. When he saw Bennett he stopped in his tracks.

"What happened?" he asked. "What the hell happened? Where's Eileen?" He hadn't put on a robe over his pajamas, which were decorated with large red hearts, probably a gift from his granddaughter.

"I was walking along the beach and I heard someone scream," Bennett explained, out of breath from the sudden exertion.

"Grandpa?" Eileen called from the kitchen wing. "Grandpa?" She came running toward him, dressed in her nightclothes. "Oh, Grandpa." She grabbed him, crying. "I've never been so scared," she sobbed.

"It's all right, it's all right," he comforted, holding her to him.

"I came downstairs to get a glass of milk and I was

185

in the kitchen and I heard a noise and I looked in here and two people were standing there at the door, and I screamed."

"I saw them, too," Bennett said.

"You woke me up when you screamed," Charlie Oliver told his granddaughter. "I leaned over and pressed the button that turns on every damn light on this property."

"It scared them," Bennett said. "I was taking a walk on the beach. When they saw me, they ran the other way. Out the front door."

"Oh, Grandpa," Eileen cried.

"Did you see who they were?" Bennett asked.

She shook her head no. "All I saw were the two people," Eileen said. "Their faces were in the dark, and they had their backs to me when they ran to the front door. But the shorter one . . ." she stopped.

"It's okay," Charlie Oliver told her.

"What about the shorter one?" Bennett asked.

"The shorter one was holding something," she said. "It flashed in the light. That's when I screamed again. When I saw that the shorter one was carrying a knife."

15

Bennett and Charlie Oliver had a drink and Eileen sat with them nursing a large glass of milk. Charlie Oliver had refused to call the police.

"They'd just show up and walk around and ask stupid questions and keep us up," he said. "As you may have guessed, I'm not too keen on the police."

"Grandpa," Eileen said warningly.

"Well, there's no harm in saying what you think and believe," Charlie said, "It's not as though I'm being rude to Mr. Bennett here, he doesn't care what I think of the police. Do you?" he asked Bennett.

The old man's eyes glittered in the light like a cat's, and Bennett wondered if perhaps Oliver had begun to suspect what Bennett's real job was. "No," Bennett reassured them, "I don't care what you think of the police. This friend of mine? Drang, on the L.A.P.D.? He's the only person I've ever known who was a policeman."

"There, you see?" Charlie Oliver told Eileen. He leaned back in his chair. "Jesus," he sighed, and swallowed half his drink. "What a world. People running around in the dead of night with knives. Jesus!"

"Did either one of you hear a car drive away when

187

they left?" Bennett asked. "I was still out on the beach."

"I didn't," Eileen said. "I was too scared to hear anything."

"I don't know whether I did or not," Oliver said. "Why'd you ask?"

"Well, it occurred to me if they didn't drive away they might be from around here someplace," Bennett said.

Charlie Oliver was staring at him. "Never occurred to me," he said, "to figure it out that way."

Bennett shrugged and threw it off. "Well," he said, "that's what happens when you read a lot of mysteries."

Charlie Oliver nodded slowly, disbelieving, but made no further comment.

"What were you doing on the beach?" Charlie Oliver asked Bennett, who had just finished his drink.

"Just walking," Bennett explained. "Just taking a walk."

"How'd you get onto the beach?" Oliver wanted to know. "There's no passageway. Houses are so close together there's been a real stink in the community about how the common ordinary folks don't get to use this natural wonder, the beach. Yet you tell me you were out for a walk. What puzzles me is, how'd you get on the beach?"

"It's a dark night," Bennett grinned. "On a dark night it's not hard to sneak through the passageway between houses, especially if one of them's empty." He couldn't tell if Charlie Oliver believed him. "It's not exactly legal, I suppose," he continued. "I suppose there's people who'd say it was trespassing." He leaned toward the old man. "You gonna report me to the police?" he asked.

"Well, no, I wouldn't do that," Charlie Oliver said, still not convinced. "But you're taking a hell of a chance, doing that. There've been robberies along here, and the people who live in these houses keep guns handy."

"I guess I was lucky," Bennett said.

"I guess you were," Oliver said, concluding the conversation.

"Well, might as well finish my walk," Bennett said. "Thanks for the drink."

Charlie Oliver shook hands with him, and Eileen attempted a curtsy while sitting in an overstuffed chair. Bennett went out the way he had come in, and once on the sand tried to remember where he'd dropped the mask. He waited until his eyes grew accustomed to the dark, then began searching. When he was ready to give up hope of ever finding it, he saw the mask lying face up in a hollow of sand. In the night it seemed as though someone had been buried while lying stretched out with only her face left uncovered.

Except for an occasional patio light, the homes along the beach were dark. Bennett walked back to the Galley house through soft sand. When he reached the stairs he put on the porcelain mask and walked up the two steps to the deck. The party was still in progress. If anything, there was more activity. He saw fewer people with masks, and recalled that once partners had been selected the masks were discarded. Which left him looking as though he were searching for a partner, he thought. He moved toward the house but was stopped by a group of people engaged in frantic activity on great beach towels that had been spread on the deck. He couldn't step over them or walk around them, they covered the area. Tiki torches had been lighted and placed in staffs attached to the deck's wood

189

railing and their flames flickered over the scene. At first glance Bennett wasn't able to differentiate the bodies; they might have been all men, or men and women, or all women. Whatever they were, they were tanned, and their hands groped and their mouths sucked and kissed and licked whatever was closest. Bennett could hear himself trying to explain to Polly where he'd been. "I think it was at an orgy," he'd tell her. "You think?" she'd say. "Don't you know what an orgy is?" And he'd have to confess that this had been his first experience. He'd heard about them, read about them, even seen photographs in the evidence files of such goings on. But standing there, trying to figure a way of getting across or around a moaning battlefield of naked bodies, he was neither impressed nor depressed by what went on. He only wondered if anyone there knew what they were doing, or cared.

First person called to him from the opposite side of the bodies. "Oh you're back. I missed you. Walk on the bench alongside the railing so you don't disturb the kiddies at play. Also it's getting very slippery through there. All juicy and sweaty."

Bennett followed directions, and walked the length of the bench until he'd passed everyone.

"I missed you," first person said. "I honestly did."

Trousers billowed as first person whirled, and turned-up shoes squeaked against the floor.

"Where were you? Don't tell me. At least you're wearing the mask so there's still time for me, I've still got a chance."

Surprisingly soft and delicate fingers reached up and grasped Bennett's hand and pulled him into another room. Here, nude men and women lay on large pillows, hands resting idly on one another's bodies, watching a giant television screen that had been placed

190

in the corner of the room. Bennett expected that they were viewing something pornographic, but when he moved to the front of the set, he saw that the replay of a football game was being shown. Sated, the guests stared without reacting, possibly unaware of the figures crashing into each other on the screen. A leaping end evaded two defending backs and caught a touchdown pass. At the game, the audience stood and cheered. In the Galley house, the naked group lying on soft pillows yawned and blinked sleepily.

"They're resting," first person whispered. "This is where they get some quiet, having had their piece." The giggle erupted from behind the mask. "In here," first person said, pulling Bennett into another room, this one furnished more expectedly, with big comfortable chairs, two sofas set at right angles to face both fireplace and the sea, and sturdy tables and lamps, only one of which was lit. First person closed the door when they were inside the room.

"Shall we touch? Don't you wonder what I am?—No," first person said. "That wouldn't be fair, would it? I know what you are, so that wouldn't be fair." With that, first person faced the opposite side of the room, and, back to Bennett, slid off the porcelain mask and the turban. "Now then," first person said, and turned. She seemed very young, not more than a child, with an impish face and oriental eyes. But they were hazel eyes, more related to her boyishly cropped blonde hair than the outline of the eye. Her face was shaped somewhat like the mask she'd been wearing, wide cheek bones, a pert nose, and a small, perfect mouth. "Surprised?" she asked. "You thought I was something else."

"Well, no," Bennett said, wondering if she was as young as she seemed to be.

"It's okay," she said, divining his thought. "I'm twenty-two years old. I look like I'm about fifteen, and that's a real kick for some people. I can see it's not a real kick for you. It worries you. Well, don't worry, I'm twenty-two. We can do anything we want, and no one's going to put you in jail for statutory rape or anything like that. If fucking is what you had in mind I'll go along with you because I really think you're terribly attractive. I have a special place in my heart and my libido for tall, dark-haired men of your age with black, intense eyes and craggy features and all those things you have going for you." She stepped close to him and put her arms around his waist. "You can take off that stupid mask," she whispered. "We know each other now. No more secrets. Just good fun."

When he didn't take off the mask she did it for him, lifting it gently from his face. The headband mussed his hair, and she dropped the mask onto a nearby chair and then straightened his part with her fingers. "You're too much," she whispered. "What'll it be? I'm accomplished. You'll see. Make believe I'm a little kid if you like."

"Listen," Bennett said, pulling away with an effort. "Did you see those two people I was following?"

She stepped back and looked at him as though someone had taken his place.

"What?" she said.

"Those two people who were here, one very tall, the other short. I don't think they were wearing masks. They looked familiar, like a couple of folks I used to know, and I followed them down the beach but they disappeared. I wondered if you'd seen them and who they were?"

"My God," she said, staring up at him. "Would you

192

the turned-up toes of her slippers stuck out from under her slender thighs. Her blonde hair, shingled like a flapper's, shone in the light of the single lamp.

No one said good-bye to Bennett when he left. He could hear the announcer excitedly describing the football game, and the cheers of the crowd on television mingled with an occasional "Oh, Jesus Christ" from the complex of bodies comingling out on the deck. He thought someone yelled "Ouch!" but it seemed out of character. He drove back to his motel, kicked off his shoes and removed his coat and tie, and sat in the single chair in the room, a hard-seated upholstered piece covered in a green-and-orange-striped material that made him dizzy when he looked at it. He flicked on the television. In progress was a movie in the Gothic mode, a film of deep shadows and sudden rain squalls, of thunder and lightning and wind-slammed shutters. There were people in it also. A pretty young woman, her dress ripped to her navel, was perpetually terrified and screamed at the slightest provocation. Before Bennett had become accustomed to the chair, she'd screeched at the top of her lungs on three separate occasions. The young man in the picture seemed friendly enough except when he thought no one was looking. At those times his normally congenial face became ugly, mean, he showed his teeth in terrible grimaces, and his eyes popped evilly. He leered, and once spittle ran down his chin. Bennett left the picture on but turned the sound off, and called Drang in Los Angeles.

"You still in La Jolla?" Drang wanted to know.

Bennett said that he was, and briefly described his evening.

"You have gall, I have to give you that," Drang said angrily. "You not only go down there when I order you not to, you spend the time at an orgy." His voice curled with contempt and envy.

"This man you've arrested," Bennett said. "What makes you so certain he's who you want?"

"He's our man." Drang sounded very positive.

"What's his connection?" Bennett asked.

"No connection is needed," Drang said. "What we have is a crazy who slashes drunks. He doesn't need a motive."

"He does in this case," Bennett said.

"You're beating a dead horse," Drang said. "I'm telling you again to get back up here. The case is solved."

"How can you be so goddam sure?" Bennett yelled. "Jesus, Drang, there are too many bits and pieces that have to be answered before I'm satisfied. How can you be so goddam sure?"

"Because our man has confessed," Drang said flatly. "That's why he was booked. Because he's confessed to those murders."

16

"You still there?" Drang asked.

Bennett was staring at the television screen. The young man had shifted to his mean mode and was stalking the girl, who'd just screamed at something or other that Bennett had missed because he'd been paying attention to Drang on the telephone.

"I'm still here," Bennett said. "Listen, Drang, I really don't want to get into an argument with you, I have a hundred and thirty-two things to do, and not numbered among them is explaining to a detective captain how confessions aren't reliable. In fact, they're to be distrusted, if the truth were known."

"I don't need lectures from you," Drang said angrily. "The chief has good reason to believe this particular confession, and if he believes it and tells the press he's got the man, then the confession is valid and we've got our man."

Bennett didn't reply. He sighed mightily, just to let Drang know that he thought the chief didn't know his whatsit from his youknowwhat.

"We've got our man, dammit!" Drang yelled. "Now you check out of wherever you are and get the hell back here! This is really serious, Fred," Drang said in

197

a less official tone, not hollering anymore. "The chief has told the press he has his man. He has told the public they may relax. The chief is going to put this sucker away for a million years, because by doing so, the chief will show the people of our proud and fair city that he knows his business, that they have the finest Chief in the world, and that'll lay the track to wherever his ambition has aimed him. Now knock it off and get back here."

"Do you think you've got the right man?" Bennett persisted.

Bennett could hear Drang's teeth grinding. Then: "You're on your own, buster," Drang said, and hung up the phone. Bennett set his instrument down slowly and carefully, as though someone in the motel might hear him. On the screen the young woman was screaming continuously. With the sound off, the effect was nightmarish. Her hands to her face in horror she opened her mouth and screamed and screamed and no one heard her, there was no one to help her, she was alone on the planet, screaming without sound, trying to make herself heard. And the young man stalked her and didn't care that she was trying to get help. (He must have known that Bennett had the sound off, which made it impossible for the young woman to be heard.)

"Oh, shit," Bennett said.

He rescued the young woman from her despair by turning off the television set. It would be nice, he thought as he did it, if everything could be solved that simply. Just turn the damn thing off. Snap. Problem solved. Click. We move onward.

He called his home.

"You all right, hon?" he asked when Polly answered.

She mumbled that she probably was. She didn't sound as though she cared whether he'd called or not.

"Listen," he said, "I'll be through here pretty soon and be back in L.A."

"The case is solved," she said wearily. "I just saw it on television. Chief Victor had a press conference. The case is solved."

"He's wrong," Bennett said.

"The chief is wrong?" Polly sounded like the disgusted straight man in a burlesque show, asking the improbable question of the comic.

"Yep," Bennett said.

"Chief Victor holds a press conference to announce that the department has their man, that the suspect is in custody, that the public need fear no more," her voice dripped with sarcasm, "but you're . . . where are you?"

"La Jolla."

"You're in La Jolla, where it's become clear to you that the chief of police of the L.A.P.D. is wrong, he's arrested the wrong man. Is that the point you're trying to make?"

"Exactly. Can I tell you why the chief's made a mistake?"

He could hear her swallow, something she did when she was trying not to yell or cry. "I don't understand you anymore," she said. Before he had a chance to reply she hung up. He couldn't believe it.

"Polly?" he shouted into the dead phone. *"Polly?"*

He jiggled the hook furiously, as though that would reconnect her. He slammed the phone down. "Son of a bitch!" he said.

He knew she'd hung up without waiting to hear his explanation because she felt that nothing he said would change her opinion, that he was chasing a figment while the case he claimed to be on was already solved. He was going to call her back, to explain his position, tell her what he had found out about the murders, lay out the questions that needed answers, none of which related to the arrest of the man in Los Angeles who'd confessed to the crimes. But it would be a useless call, he knew, even if she answered the phone and listened to him. Because she felt that he'd do almost anything to prove the importance of his work in the department. He'd go against the chief, against Drang, against her. And she'd be right. He had to admit it. Like now, he reminded himself. He was on to something, he didn't yet know what, but he was absolutely certain that he was right and the chief and Drang and even Polly were wrong.

He laid out the questions in his mind. If the arrested man was the guilty person, where had he gotten the mask? And had Drang found a mask on this person, or in his belongings?

Why did the murderer wear a porcelain mask?

Why had the most recent murder been committed out of the downtown section of the city?

Who were the two people Bennett had followed from the Galley house down the beach to Charlie Oliver's house? If he were to go on physical descriptions alone, he'd suspect they were Franny Harris and Sonny. Why had they left a box of masks for L. George? L. George was dead.

Why did Charlie Oliver think his daughter Gwen had been murdered when the police called it a suicide? And did that event have any connection with everything else that had been happening?

Bennett poured himself a drink and got ready for bed. He turned on the television, and for an instant thought he was watching the climactic scene of the picture he'd just turned off: a scene in which the evil young man at last catches the terrified young woman and eats her up, with fries on the side and a withered ripe olive. The camera pulled back in time for Bennett to identify a hamburger commercial that had begun with an extreme close-up of a man's mouth and jaws biting into something that might have been the terrified girl with catsup on her. It was the french fries which gave it away, Bennett decided. Once he saw the french fries he knew it was a commercial. Most feature-length pictures didn't use french fries.

Another movie started. This one was about some nice, decent, neighborhood girls whose maximum garments were bikinis, which they wore everywhere they went. Bennett watched the luscious young bodies bounce around gardens and beaches and cars and tennis courts and jogging paths, finished his drink, turned off the television set and the lights, and went to sleep.

In the morning he called Drang again.

"You may be right," he told him. "You may have the right man."

"We do have the right man," Drang said flatly.

"But I've stumbled onto something that should be of interest to the department. It might turn out to be another matter entirely, but it is something that should be pursued."

"What is it?" Drang didn't sound particularly interested but he'd slept well and he was being polite.

"The death of Gwen Oliver Thompson," Bennett said. "According to her father, it was an unsolved murder that remains unsolved because information that could have pointed the finger of guilt went to the grave with L. George Galley. Have I got that straight?"

"No. The coroner determined it was a suicide. I told you that."

"But suppose it wasn't?" Bennett asked. "Suppose

her father is right. After all, *probable suicide* is what the coroner said, have I got that straight?"

"Yes." Drang didn't sound terribly interested.

"A probable suicide makes me nervous," Bennett said. "It causes me to ask questions. Questions such as how L. George Galley died, since he's the person who was supposed to have information on the Thompson woman's death. When did he die? What caused his death? Is it in any way connected to the case we're working on back there. . . ."

"This case is solved," Drang interrupted.

"Yeah. Well, the off chance is what I'm concerned with. Listen, Drang, if you can get me all the particulars on the death of L. George Galley, why that'll ease my mind, I won't wake up in the middle of the night thinking I let an innocent nut go to prison for life because I didn't bother to check out a couple of three things, and I'll come back to house and hearth and department and you won't hear another peep out of me. Cross my heart and hope to die."

Drang had cooled off during the night. "Fair enough," he said. "You understand, I'm sure, that I wasn't trying to put a stop to your activities. You're a damn good officer . . ."

"Thanks. I appreciate your confidence."

". . . and I wouldn't want to stifle your work in any way." Drang was beginning to sound as though he was speaking at a lunch of the J.C. Boosters. He must have heard himself, because he wound up the speech with a few more qualified accolades, and then advised Bennett he'd get back to him soonest. Bennett gave Drang the motel phone number and hung up.

He showered and shaved and found among the items the management had stashed in the slender desk a card that advised that the adjoining coffee shop would be

202

happy to bring breakfast to the guest's room. The service wasn't provided for lunch or dinner. Also among the papers were laundry lists, postcards, and a single sheet of stationery on which someone had written, in a drunken scrawl, "Dear Sweetheart can you ever forgive me for being such a fool. If only you knew . . ."

Bennett called the phone number on the breakfast card and ordered a bear-claw heated and coffee. When the woman at the other end of the phone maternally asked whether he didn't want fruit juice since it was fresh-squeezed, Bennett was intimidated into ordering juice. Drang called back as he was finishing his second cup of coffee.

"I have the complete file," he said. "As we've discussed, the report on the Thompson woman was probable suicide. The last person to have seen her alive was L. George Galley, whose only statement was that they were friends, had run into each other on the afternoon of her death, had chatted for a while, and then he'd gone about his business. Her father doubted the suicide theory and pressured the department, but there was no evidence of anything but suicide."

"What about Galley?" Bennett wanted to know.

"He's dead, as you know. He and two friends went fishing. Small power boat. Heavy seas. Somehow, the two survivors don't know how, the boat overturned. The two survivors were picked up within an hour— there were several boats out that day. Galley was never seen again. Presumed drowned."

"How far out were they?" Bennett asked.

"Mile or two," Drang said. "The La Jolla police don't question that he drowned, if that's what you're getting at, and they've had more experience with what can happen in those waters than I have."

"Yeah," Bennett conceded. "Well, thanks."

"Hey! Wait a minute!" Drang yelled.

"Yes?"

"This is it, Fred. Get your ass back here. I've satisfied your curiosity. I can't say you're still on the skidrow case when we've got the guilty party in jail. I'm going to have to stop covering for you."

"I think there might be a connection between skid row and La Jolla," Bennett patiently explained. "And that's what I'm trying to find out. There's no need to cover, for God's sake. I'm working on a case, which is what I'm paid to do. I'll be back when I complete this portion of the investigation." He liked the way it sounded and was proud of how he'd put it.

Drang breathed heavily on the other end of the phone.

"Drang?" Bennett called into the phone. "Are you still there?"

"You are one rotten sonofabitch," Drang said, his voice trembling with rage. "You are one of the worst examples of a human being I have ever heard of. You are the crappiest officer it has ever been my unfortunate bad luck to have worked with. . . ."

"You were complimenting me less than half an hour ago," Bennett reminded him.

"I'm no longer covering," Drang said abruptly. "You're on your goddam own. Whatever happens you did it to yourself." The phone went dead.

This time Bennett knew it was for real. Usually, when he and Drang disagreed on something, Bennett could cajole and con, and finally Drang would go along with him. But it was different now. Now, it was clear, Drang had to side with the chief because the chief believed he had the case wrapped up. *No more cover*, Drang had said, which meant there was no doubt which side he was on. Had to be on.

Just as Bennett was compelled to go forward. The questions he'd been asking himself were still unanswered, so it didn't matter if Drang told him to lay off, or if the chief claimed the case was solved, or if Polly thought he was malingering in La Jolla. He thought otherwise. And he could no more have walked away from it at that point than he could have flown to the moon on a firecracker. Bennett was a good cop because once he was onto something he followed it until all questions were answered. The only difference between what was happening to him now and what had happened to him before was that this time it could cost him his wife and his job.

Even realizing that, he couldn't call it off.

He found the address of the public library in the battered phone book in his room, asked directions of the desk clerk, and drove to a low building, the replica of an early California home, built on a rise of ground beneficently located between the hills that rose behind it and the sea that lay below it. In the reference room Bennett went through the newspaper files, beginning with the issues of the week before, and working his way backward through the papers until he found the obituary notice for L. George Galley. "Tragically lost at sea," read the obit. "Survived by his beloved wife Theresa and adored son Lester. Will be sorely missed." Two days before was the news story. L. George Galley, local motion-picture producer (the journalist had wisely omitted any reference to what picture L. George had produced) had gone fishing with two cronies, Alfred "Whitey" Whitford, and Leon Fell, in Whitey's outboard. It was a windy, choppy day, and the seas were running. An unexpected squall blew in and the boat was swamped by the sudden heavy seas. Whitey and Leon Fell had hung on until they were picked up by another fishing boat, but L. George was never seen again. Pillar of the community, loved and respected by friends and neighbors, active in local charities, and so on. No mention in the news story of wife or son. Bennett returned the papers to the file, found a phone book near a stack of booths near the restrooms, and got an address for Alfred K. Whitford. He thanked the librarian, who was reading something secretly and blushed when he spoke to her, and left.

He stopped at a gas station for directions, and ten minutes later was parked in a modest neighborhood of homes and businesses in front of a small shop on which was lettered, "Whitey's Health Foods and Vitamins." The windows, one on either side of the door, displayed vitamins, strands of dried seaweed, and shriveled objects that might have been sections of the carcasses of creatures who no longer roamed the earth. Also on view were framed photographs of men and women holding aloft dead fish and wearing army fatigues, ancient tweed jackets, and foul weather gear so old it could no longer protect against drizzle. Bennett assumed that the man who appeared most often in these photographs was the proprietor of Whitey's Health Foods, Alfred K. Whitford himself. Through the window he saw the same man, standing behind a counter at the rear of the store, watching him, a ruddy heavyset fellow with a Toby mug face. Bennett entered.

"Yessir, can I help you?" the gentleman in the rear of the store asked.

"Whitey around?" Bennett asked.

"You're speaking to him and looking at him," Whitey said. "Alfred K. Whitford, known to one and all as Whitey."

A woman entered the store from a rear room, a heavyset woman with blonde hair done up in ringlets and curls. She wore jeans, as her husband did, and a Pendleton wool shirt that had been through many dozens of washings.

"And this," Whitey announced, "is my better half, the love of my life, Mrs. Alfred K. Whitford, known to one and all as Baby."

Bennett said hello and Baby smiled and said "How d'do."

"And how can I be of service?" Whitey asked. "From the look of you, you're a fine, strong young fella who possibly isn't getting enough of the trace elements or the scarcer vitamins, the higher-numbered B's, and the oxygenating attenuates that allow them to absorb directly into the bloodstream without having to go a mile and a half down the road to the first left turn, if you follow me."

Bennett didn't but said he did.

"We have a special, this week only, for a complex that is combined with garlic and seaweed for easier digestion, since the lower stomach and upper bowel must also be considered in these matters. It comes in a tablet . . ."

Baby had reached under the counter and now held in a piece of Kleenex an enormous pill that seemed more appropriate for horse colic. She held it out for Bennett's examination.

". . . a tablet which," Whitey continued, "is taken once a day after a meal that should include pulp of some sort. We recommend dried fruit peelings."

Bennett said it looked interesting but he'd have to think about it. "I hate to clutter up my system without giving it some warning first," he told Whitey and Baby. "You know better than I do how your system can get shocked and surprised when you do something to it that it doesn't expect. Eating grapes while showering is a good example."

They looked at him suspiciously.

"Of course," he continued, "you don't have to worry about that in La Jolla."

Whitey and Baby agreed eating grapes in the shower had never been a problem in La Jolla.

"Tell you why I'm here," Bennett said. "L. George has been telling me for years about you two, and then I was up in L.A. and I heard what had happened. My God, it knocked me for a loop and I came down here first shot out of the barrel to ask you what the hell's going on?" He turned quickly to Baby. "My sincere apologies for that language," he said. "It's just when I'm upset."

"Apology accepted," she cooed over her chins.

"Well, bless my soul," Whitey said, as though he'd just stepped out of a Dickens story. "L. George often mentioned Baby and me?"

"While in my presence it was more than often," Bennett said. "L. George had a genuine love and affection for the two of you. My God!" he said. "What could have happened to the dear man?"

"We were fishing," Whitey said. "L. George and Leon Fell and me." He stopped. "He ever tell you about Leon Fell?"

"He might have mentioned his name," Bennett conceded, "but if he did it was only in a very casual way."

"Oh, yeah, of course. You see, Baby and me were the ones who were real close to L. George. Leon Fell, he just sort of came along, you know. To help out with handling the boat and so on and so forth. The newspaper said he was a crony, which is definitely not true. Leon Fell was no more a crony of L. George's than a complete stranger would have been, if you understand what I'm saying."

"I understand," Bennett said. "Completely."

"Well, it was one of them days when the wind is blowing and the seas are up, but I will tell you that the squall line that hit us was completely unexpected. Even though his arm was in that sling, L. George was handling the boat. We'd just pulled up our lines and we were going to try another spot because the fishing wasn't all that good—some mackerel was about it. And somehow we got ourselves running sideways to some pretty big seas, and I yelled to L. George and he yelled back that it was all right, he was going to head into it, I shouldn't worry. And then she hit us. I mean hit us! Flipped us over like we were a piece of board, you know. Just flipped us right over. I came up on the far side of the boat, and Leon Fell came up near the stern. We never did see L. George. What I believe happened is that when the boat flipped over that way something struck L. George on the head. I believe he was a dead man before he hit the water. And of course with that hurt arm and all he couldn't swim worth . . ."

He stopped. Telling the story, which he'd probably done a hundred times since the accident, had left him drained, his eyes misted. Baby walked to a water cooler and filled a paper cup, which she handed him. He thanked her and drank it.

Bennett let him catch his breath, then said, "What a terrible experience."

Whitey nodded gravely.

"It was awful," Baby said.

"It must have been," Bennett sympathized.

Whitey continued nodding, the memory of his friend's death engulfing him in grief.

209

"How're Theresa and Lester taking it?" Bennett asked solicitously.

It was as though he'd dropped a stink bomb in the center of the shop. Baby's nose crinkled with disgust. Whitey's eyebrows rose to touch his hairline, creating a corduroy forehead.

"Theresa and Lester?" Whitey asked. "You know Theresa and Lester?"

Bennett backed and filled. "Only to hear L. George mention their names," he said quickly. "I've never met them."

"Well I should hope not," Whitey indignantly said. "I should hope that a friend of L. George's didn't have a close relationship with those two." He turned to Baby, who made a face that signified agreement.

"Do they live down here?" Bennett asked. "L. George never said. He told me about them, mentioned their names now and then, but he never said where they lived."

"She lives down here," Whitey sniffed. "No one knows what happened to Lester."

"Lester's no good, you know," Baby confided.

"I didn't know that," Bennett said.

"Oh yes," Baby said emphatically. "Lester's no good. Never was," she said.

"I just feel I should pay my respects to her," Bennett said. "I did know her late husband. It wouldn't be right for me to be down here and not drop in to pay my respects, bring her some flowers."

"You're a good man," Baby said. "Isn't he?" she asked her husband.

Whitey nodded mutely. He found a scrap of paper on the counter, and a pencil. "You have her address?" he asked his wife.

Baby located a ledger lying alongside a glass apothe-

210

cary jar large enough to have held Ali Baba and the forty thieves. She thumbed through it. "Her last address was on Monte Cordo," she announced. "Twelve, is the number. That's if she hasn't moved," she sneered.

"She'd never move," her husband replied, writing down the address, then handing Bennett the paper. "She'd stay there forever if she could."

"A woman's place is with her husband," Baby said. "She's never learned that."

Her husband nodded sagely. "Truer words," he said, "were never spoke."

"How would I get to Monte Cordo?" Bennett asked Whitey.

"I would suggest the best way's to go back down the hill to Crescent, which is the curving street you crossed when you drove up here. Take a right on Crescent down almost to the water's edge, where you'll see Monte Cordo. It's a private street. Sign says 'Not a Through Street. No Exit.' That's on your right. Take Monte Cordo to its end. Number 12 is at the end of the street. If number 12 wasn't there you'd drive right into the water."

"Thanks for your help," Bennett said. "It's no wonder L. George thought so highly of the two of you. You're champs."

They thanked him. They liked being called champs.

"I got to tell you," Whitey said as he opened the door for Bennett, "that this is a very decent thing you're doing. Most people wouldn't have tiddly-boo to do with Theresa. But she is widowed, and this is very decent what you're doing. God bless you, sir, for what you're doing to honor L. George's memory."

Bennett accepted the compliment with grace. Then,

211

casually, he said: "You mentioned something about L. George's arm being in a sling."

"Oh yes," Whitey said.

"Last time I saw him it was all right," Bennett said. "What happened?"

"Got a terrible cut," Whitey said. "While he was up in Los Angeles he told us he had an accident. Got this cut on his arm . . ." he touched his own forearm to illustrate. "Deep cut. That's why his arm was in a sling."

"He tell you how it happened?" Bennett asked.

"Didn't say. No. So I don't know did someone cut him or did he cut himself."

17

Although he hadn't hurt anyone, Bennett reminded himself, he had done some fibbing and stroking to get information from Whitey and Baby. It was an accepted part of his job, he knew. Not a part he particularly liked, but an absolutely necessary part that made him feel like a fake and a fraud.

Even though he had a facility for it, Polly hated that he was so glib. She'd accuse him of conning her to get what he wanted, of not being entirely truthful. She had never called him a liar because he never really lied. He'd stretch the truth, test its limits, but never exceed them. He did what he had to do, within the limits of propriety he'd set for himself long ago, before Vietnam, probably before the deaths of his parents, since his personal codes were so firmly established.

He followed Whitey's directions, enjoying a day that could only be called glorious. The morning sun sparkled on the sea below. Three-foot waves rolled toward the shore, piled up on the sand, and softly crashed, their curve green in the sunlight, the spray foaming around the legs of brave souls who were enjoying the beach on a November day. To his north the square concrete buildings of the Scripps Institute of Oceanography were nearly hidden by a cliff face.

He turned right on Monte Cordo, passing the "No Exit" sign, and drove down a narrow street lined with castle-like homes. At the foot of the grade he stopped at a stone and ironwork barrier that walled a great pink monstrosity built by someone who had here proved that bushels of money and good taste do not necessarily go hand in hand. The building seemed to be constructed of afterthoughts: turrets added, wings built on, walls crenelated for protection against the hordes who might someday attack out of the sea or down from the hills. Clipped hedges and geometrically exact walks and flowerbeds made up the garden portion of the property. There was not a curve in view; everything was angular—sharply cut corners, perfect triangles, never a soft line. It might have been a fortress still in the control of the military. And when he looked, sure enough, Bennett saw two flagpoles on the south side of the house, and from them flew the flags of the State of California and the United States of America.

Someone had seen him coming, for as he stopped the great wrought-iron gates squealed open, dropping bits of rusted iron from hinges rarely used. He drove onto the property along a gravel drive unmarked by car tracks or footprints, and parked under a jacaranda that still bore a few lacy green leaves, faded from the sun and the salt spray. Behind him the gates rattled, ground to a halt, then began closing. Bennett slid out of his car, assumed the expression of one about to enter a house in mourning, and tapped the front bell. From within the house he heard a soft chime. A mockingbird, white wing patches blazing, yelled at him, swooped past his head, and landed on the highest branch of jacaranda. He was watching the bird when the door opened.

"Yes, please?"

He turned to face a tiny Oriental woman wearing a half-smile on an otherwise impassive face. Her black hair had been braided and the braids tied over the top of her head, so that she seemed to be wearing crochet-work in place of a hat. Her starched apricot-colored uniform reached just below her knees.

"Mrs. Galley, if she's receiving guests," Bennett said, his right hand touching his heart.

"Who is calling?" the Oriental woman wanted to know.

"Mr. Bennett," Bennett said, keeping his voice quiet and respectful. "An old friend of her late husband's, come to pay his respects."

"Show him in," a woman called from inside the house.

"This way," the Oriental woman said.

Bennett followed her through enormous, silent rooms, furnished with what appeared to be antiques from the court of the Sun King, and looking as foolish as fine French furniture can when overpowered by heavy doors and thick beams and massive paintings of cupids floating through clouds, holding hands, smiling beatifically, entwined with garlands of a flower Bennett had never seen before. It resembled a tulip but grew on a rose's thorny branches, and was the color of mud. After they'd passed through four rooms, Bennett could see light from the beach falling through large, modern windows that faced the sea. Enormous wicker chairs, all aimed at the view, were scattered throughout the room, so that it resembled the setting of any spy story whose locale was India or the South Pacific.

"What was your name?" the invisible woman asked.

215

"Frederick Bennett," he said, trying to figure out which chair she was sitting in.

"You were a friend of my husband's?" she asked.

"Yes, ma'am, and I've come to offer my condolences at his recent demise."

He couldn't hear her laugh, but he could see that the chair closest to the window was swaying. He walked to it, and looked down at a very thin, elegant woman in her late fifties, dressed in white duck slacks and a cotton sweater as pale a blue as her eyes. She was very tan. Her hair, streaked with gray, was pulled back tightly. She was attractive despite what should have been an ugly face, prominent nose separating close-set, pale blue eyes, thin lips painted scarlet, and yellowing teeth now completely exposed as she laughed. "Recent demise," she laughed. "Oh dear."

Bennett stood silently, looking down at her.

"Sit down, Mr. Bennett," she said.

Bennett sat beside her. "I've come to offer my condolences," he repeated.

"I don't know why you've come," she said. "But I know it wasn't to offer your condolences. Why would anyone be sorry that L. George Galley was dead?"

"He had many friends," Bennett said somberly, and wondered how many. Not more than a handful, he guessed.

Mrs. Galley leaned forward and looked at him more closely. "What is it you want?" she asked directly.

Below and to his left, on the sand, Bennett thought he saw L. George's beach house. Mrs. Galley noticed where he was looking.

"He spent more time there than here," she said. "My husband was an attractive guttersnipe. I'm a Heatherton." Simple statements, regally spoken. *A woman of iron*, Bennett thought.

216

ing there's an estrangement between
Lester?" Bennett asked.

wn conclusions." Her eyes were open
t at the beach house. Harsh lines had
r face, pressing the thin lips more
a scarlet slash underlining the sharp

im? Speak to him? Hear from him?"

r head to each question, small quick
energy wasted on the prodigal son, not
on of his mother's head.

where he is now?" Bennett asked.
include his comments in your story?
she said.

ly quote him in the most favorable
uggested.

hange anything after I've okayed the

nctuation," Bennett promised.

t to give Bennett the address when she
ething else. "Why are you anxious to
Lester?" she asked.

inion of his father," he said.

urse." The hands once again were
, fingers touching. "Lester, when I last
Los Angeles. He had taken rooms in a
Northern. I don't have the address."

t," Bennett said. "How long ago was

l," she said. "I'm sure if he's no longer
ave left a forwarding address. My son
rn his bridges to me. We disagree on
y son and I, but we stand together in
my husband."

"Are you from the press?" she asked.

Bennett didn't say yes or no. He squirmed uneasily in his chair and let her decide.

"I thought you were," she said, confirming her own opinion. "I can usually tell. You give yourselves away. You lie badly. Which I suppose is paradoxical, considering the sort of stories you write, made up of whole cloth." She leaned back in her chair, touched her fingertips together, and placed them at her thin lips. "I suppose you wonder why I didn't divorce my husband long ago. His reputation was such that most women would have. My church would not allow it, nor could I personally condone it. Till death, we swore. Through sickness and all the rest, we swore. To love and to cherish. He did none of the above." She lowered her hands and looked at Bennett. "Aren't you taking notes?" she asked.

"It's not necessary," Bennett told her.

"Ahh, you're one of those with an absolute memory," she said. She was a woman who had accepted the fact, rightly or wrongly, that she was smarter and cleverer and quicker than anyone else, especially if the someone else was a man; and so she read into someone else's mind and speech motives and answers that did not necessarily reflect what the other person was thinking or about to say. "Well, I don't trust your memory," she said with a tight smile. "I'll need to approve your story before it's printed. Understood?"

Bennett agreed it was understood. He knew that lonely people wanted someone to talk to, and he recognized that Mrs. Galley was a lonely woman, sitting before a window on the sea side of her house where she'd looked down and watched her husband live his other life.

"You said you were a Heatherton," he prompted her.

"My great-great-grandfather owned this land," she said, her hands and arms reaching toward the beach and the house and the hills behind the house. "The Heathertons are an old family. My husband had no money to speak of. My husband took what I gave him and played at being many things." She studied Bennett once more. "You knew my husband because you'd interviewed him," she guessed. "Probably when he was making that dreadful film, what was it called?"

" 'The Dungeons of Hell County,' " Bennett said.

"Yes. Exactly," she said, pleased with herself. "You see?" she said. "I have a facility. I can pretty well read people. I read my husband shortly after we were married. He fooled me at first, but then I was able to read him. A guttersnipe, as I've said. An unfeeling person. I was deceived, at the beginning of the relationship, but I quickly caught on. All the affairs since, I've known about them. Did he think I would give him a divorce? Of course not. Besides he didn't want a divorce, and if he had I wouldn't have given it to him. My husband knew when he had a good thing. As for me, I learned early in my life that a contract is a contract, an agreement sworn to by the participating parties. Marriage is the most sacred of these. My sainted mother taught me that."

Her eyes drifted toward the house on the beach. "He was a childish man. Not childlike, mind you. Childish. Spoiled. But I was able to keep the reins on him. He was frisky, but I kept control of him."

"Did your husband have a great many affairs?" Bennett asked in his best reportorial tone.

"A very good angle," she complimented him. "Yes, he had many many affairs, all of them meaningless.

218

Medically, and you can
ities, medically my hus
Juan complex, it wa
women. Without that
a person. He suffered
closing her eyes sudder

"It must have beer
man like that," Bennet

"Yes."

"But you bore it."

"He was my husban
illness in no way miti
anything it strengthene
gether once more, and
as if in this way she co

"What of the women

She nodded. "I've t
all, their own free cho
If they didn't immedi
out."

"How?"

She didn't understar

"How did they find

"Oh I saw that they
made sure they knew
going to divorce him
contract in God's eye
band, not their's. My

"Your son," Bennet

Her eyes closed aga

"His father spoke o
Is that his name?"

"Yes," she said col
mother and son. Noth

"Are you
you and you

"Draw yo
again, starin
appeared o
tightly toget
features.

"Do you
Bennett aske

She shook
movements,
even in the n

"Do you k

"So you
No, thank yo

"I would
light," Benne

"You won
story?"

"Not even

She was a
thought of s
talk to my . .

"I want his

"Yes, of
pressed toget
heard, lived
hotel. The Gr

"I can fin
this?"

"I can't re
there, he will
doesn't ever
many things,
our loathing o

"How old is your son?" Bennett asked.

"Lester is . . ." she closed her eyes. "Lester is now twenty-two years old. He has a birthday very soon. He was born on Thanksgiving Day, and we gave thanks, his father and I. We gave thanks." She shuddered delicately.

"Do you know Gwen Thompson?" Bennett asked.

"One of my husband's women," she said. "Why do you ask?"

"I met her father," he said.

"Who is her father?"

"A man named Charlie Oliver."

"No," she said. "I don't believe I know Charlie Oliver."

"He has a home on the beach," Bennett said. "South of your husband's beach house."

"I don't know the beach people," she said. "They only recently built their homes."

Bennett thanked her for her time, promised on his mother's good name that he'd let Mrs. Galley see his article for approval and corrections before it was published, and with that she escorted him through the great rooms, immaculately kept and unlived in. Bennett doubted if they were used except as passageways from one place in the house to another.

As she opened the front door she said, "You haven't been absolutely honest with me. You're not with a large magazine."

Bennett was too stunned to reply.

"You're a freelance writer," she told him. "You hope to sell this story to a magazine. If you were already employed you would have given me one of your business cards. Is that correct?"

"Yes, Mrs. Galley, you're correct. You're a very astute woman," he said.

She already knew that she was, so she agreed. "I'm not easy to fool," she said. "My husband succeeded, but only for a very short time." She held out her hand. "Good-bye," she said.

Bennett shook hands with her, echoed her good-bye, and drove off. In his rearview mirror, as the iron gate swung open to let him out, he saw her standing in the doorway, slim and elegant, the widow of a man she'd called a guttersnipe.

He drove back to the public library. As he entered, the woman reading the trashy book looked up and smiled guiltily.

"Hello again," she said.

Bennett held out his index finger and stroked it with the opposite index finger and mouthed "shame on you." She laughed. He walked back to the research room, found the Los Angeles phone books, and began looking for Salvatore Thompson. Not in Central Los Angeles. Not in the Western section, or the Northern and San Fernando Valley sections. He found a Salvatore Thompson in the Pasadena section, copied the address and phone number, and left.

As he walked out the front door the librarian waved good-bye without looking up from her book. Bennett returned to his motel and reached his room as a pretty young Mexican woman was vacuuming her way out the door.

"All done," she said cheerily, snatching the vacuum cord out of the outlet nearest the door.

"Thank you," Bennett said, as she left and he entered. The room smelled of disinfectant. He opened the windows to encourage fresh air, sat on the side of the bed, picked up the phone, and told the switchboard he wanted area code 213, and the number 555-6525.

Connections were made, the phone was picked up, and a friendly young woman said: "Hello there."

"Sal at home?" Bennett asked.

"He's at work, dummy," the woman said. "Who's calling?"

"I'm not sure he'd remember the name," Bennett said.

"Let's give it a try," she said.

"Frederick Bennett."

"You must go way back."

"Oh yes."

"To Gwen?"

"To Gwen."

He could hear her breathing. "She keeps popping up," she said, "like a rotten apple, as the saying goes. Is that to be the subject of your conversation with Sal?"

"I'd like it to be," Bennett said. "I think I might be able to make him feel better about that episode in his life."

"I'll vote for that," she said. "You know Sal and I didn't even meet until after she was gone. The fact that Sal and I got married didn't have anything to do with Gwen dying that way. That was a whole separate thing."

"That's what I thought," Bennett said.

"Well, you'd better believe it," she said. "And you know as well as I do there wasn't anything left there anyway. It was long gone. Over and done with. Washed up."

"Well, sure," Bennett agreed.

"Okay," she said. "Just so you know that."

Bennett wondered why she was so defensive about her marriage to Salvatore Thompson. He was normally suspicious of anyone who protested too much, or who volunteered a defense before any accusations had been made.

"Call Sal at dinner time," she said. "He usually gets home at about six or six-thirty, it depends on that freeway. Now that the Dodgers aren't playing it's not too tough on him. When the Dodgers have an evening game that freeway is the bitter end. Poor Sal. I really feel for him then. He gets tired so easily since the accident."

"Accident?" Bennett asked.

"Oh you really haven't been in touch," she said. "Sal was minding his own business one night a couple of weeks ago and some nut tried to kill him, tried to cut my husband's throat. Can you imagine?"

18

Salvatore Thompson lived in a small frame house on the northern edges of Pasadena, where the foothills begin to slope up to the San Gabriel mountains. Bennett had checked out of his Là Jolla motel after his phone conversation with Thompson's wife and driven back to Los Angeles. He'd called Thompson from a gas station, getting him just as he walked into the house.

"Bennett?" Thompson had said. "I don't remember anyone named Fred Bennett."

"It's about your late wife, Gwen," Bennett had said.

"Oh, shit," Thompson had said.

"Would you like to bury her for good?" Bennett had asked.

And Salvatore Thompson had said that was precisely what he'd like to do. Bury Gwen and all that had happened between them for good and all. Write "The End" to those years. Close the damn book.

And so now Bennett drove up to the Thompson house. A small weedy lawn separated house from street, and as Bennett walked along the cracked concrete path that split the lawn in half, the front door opened and a tall, husky man appeared. He wore a business shirt, the tie removed and the sleeves rolled halfway, suit trousers and Indian moccasins. His receding hair was reddish, topping strong, heavy features.

"Bennett?" he asked.

"How are you?" Bennett said. "You must be Salvatore Thompson."

"Come on in," Thompson said.

Bennett entered a small house, well kept and simply furnished.

A striking young woman, the planes of her face suggesting exotic forebears, appeared in the doorway that led from living room to kitchen. Bennett could smell food cooking.

"Am I interrupting your dinner?" he asked.

"Not for half an hour," the woman said.

"This is my wife Margaret," Thompson said.

They greeted each other, and Thompson gestured Bennett into a chair. Margaret Thompson sat on the sofa opposite him.

"Get you a drink?" Thompson asked.

"Only if you're having one," Bennett said.

"Maybe a little wine," Thompson said. Three glasses stood ready on a small table near the kitchen, with an open wine bottle beside them. Thompson poured the wine, passed the glasses, and sat beside his wife.

"I'm talking to you because you said we could really bury Gwen," he told Bennett. "I don't know who you are, or what you do, but I'm willing to listen." His wife reached and touched his arm. "We're willing to listen," he said.

Bennett was struck by the simplicity of the house and the people who lived in it. After seeing Charlie Oliver's Bel Air estate and La Jolla beach house, he'd expected that Oliver's daughter would have married someone wealthier than Salvatore Thompson.

"What's your interest in this?" Thompson asked.

"You police? Not that it makes any difference. I talked to the police when it all happened, I could talk to them again, if I had some assurance it would end the matter."

"I believe this conversation will end the matter," Bennett said. "Tell me about your accident."

Thompson looked surprised. "I thought you wanted to talk about Gwen."

"I do," Bennett explained. "But I was curious about your accident. Your wife mentioned it on the phone and I wondered how you were feeling."

"Pretty good," Thompson said. He touched his right arm above his elbow. Through the shirt Bennett saw the bulge of a bandage. "Cut me to the bone."

"They find who did it?" Bennett asked.

"No. If you're a cop, you'll discover I don't think much about the efficiency of you guys."

Bennett didn't comment. In his present temper he would have had to agree. "How'd it happen?" he asked.

Thompson shrugged. "I worked late one night, couple of weeks ago I guess it was." He turned to his wife for confirmation. She nodded. "Damn car quit on me halfway home. Here in Pasadena, for God's sake. I went looking for a phone booth. Found one, called Margaret, and told her where I was and she said she'd come and pick me up. I was walking back to my car when I was jumped. Damn knife got me here . . ." he touched the arm. "It was like a razor. Cut through my jacket, my shirt, damn near amputated the arm. I fell down. Luckily a car was driving by, headlights picked us out, me and the person who cut me. Cutter ran like a rabbit, the car chasing him. I lay there. God, it hurt. I finally got up and headed toward my car."

"I found him sitting on the curb, holding his poor

arm," Margaret Thompson said. "He'd lost a lot of blood. I drove him to the emergency hospital. We made out the reports, and that was the end of it."

"Well, not quite," Thompson said. "A young cop came by the next morning and asked what I'd seen of my assailant, and I told him what I could, and that was the end of it," he corrected his wife.

"What'd you tell him?" Bennett asked.

"That I never did see the man's face. I'm guessing it was a man because of the strength necessary to cut me that way. Slight wiry figure, dressed all in black, from what I could see."

The hairs on the back of Bennett's neck rose.

"You didn't see this person's face?" he asked.

"No. It was dark, and by the time I realized I'd been cut, and turned around, whoever it was was off and running. Scared away by the car."

"Was your assailant wearing a mask?" Bennett asked.

"A mask?" Thompson's face flushed. "Why the hell would someone be wearing a mask?" he sputtered.

Bennett shrugged without comment.

Thompson turned to his wife.

"Tell him," she said.

"I don't know," Thompson said. "I told Margaret, when the headlights of that car hit us, and this person ran off, I thought I saw something shine in the light. I couldn't figure out what it was. Still haven't been able to. Then you ask about a mask. What kind of mask are you talking about?"

"I've heard of cases where attackers sometimes disguise themselves," was all Bennett said.

Thompson wasn't sure if that was really all there was to the question, but he let it pass.

Bennett said, "I'll tell you what I've been told about

Gwen, and perhaps you can straighten it out for me, and perhaps that'll be the end of it."

"Okay," Thompson agreed.

"I know some of this will remind you of things you'd rather forget . . ." Bennett said tentatively.

"It's not going to go away just because nobody talks about it," Thompson said. "Margaret knows that Gwen got involved with a guy named L. George Galley, a little guy. . . ." He stuttered for an instant, as if remembering something about L. George Galley. Then he said: "She had an affair with him. I found out about it after it had been going on for nearly a year. She said she'd break it off. Turns out she didn't."

"How'd she die?" Bennett asked.

"What's your information? That she was killed? Has the old man fed you that? He finds it impossible to accept the fact that his daughter, the mother of his grandchild, was begging L. George Galley on her hands and knees to take her back, under any conditions—she'd do anything—and L. George turned his back on her. So she killed herself. Bloody mess."

The memory clouded his eyes. Margaret touched his arm reassuringly.

"I've told you my feelings about cops. Gwen's death is partly responsible. They carried the case as a possible homicide just because that old sonofabitch kept hammering at them. I guess they figured it was easier to do that than argue."

"How'd she die?" Bennett asked.

Thompson looked surprised. "Don't you know?" he asked. "Got in a tub full of water and cut her wrists."

"And the police doubted it was suicide?"

"For a while, yeah. They thought maybe L. George had murdered her. All stuff the old man was feeding them. He's a tenacious old bastard."

229

"How would Galley have committed the murder?" Bennett asked.

"As fed to everyone by the old man, L. George Galley saw her get ready for her bath, and since she'd repeatedly rejected him, murdered her by cutting her wrists."

"And she just sat there in the bathtub and let him do it?" Bennett asked.

"That'll give you an idea of how much trouble the old man can cause."

"I understand your wife spent a lot of time in La Jolla." Bennett said. "Any particular reason?"

Thompson looked uncomfortable. "I've never made a lot of money," he said. "I do some acting, commercials; I sell things; whatever brings in a buck. Right now I'm almost in real estate," he said dryly. "Anyhow, her father spoiled my wife. He gave her a taste for the finer things, especially those finer things that cost a hell of a lot of money. Gwen and I and the baby had an apartment in Hollywood, but she wasn't really ever there. She and the baby were at the old man's Bel Air house or his La Jolla beach house. They were there because my wife liked being places where people waited on her, and it was comfortable, and where she was readily available if L. George wanted to spend some time with her."

He sank back on the couch and rubbed his eyes. Then he finished his glass of wine, slowly, as if he were drinking medicine.

"You said the purpose of this talk would be to bury Gwen for the last and final time. Is she buried?"

"I think so," Bennett said.

"Does that do it for you then?" Thompson asked, preparing to rise.

"Do you see your daughter?" Bennett asked.

"Yes," Thompson replied. "Not often enough. But I can't afford the lawyers I'd need to keep fighting the old man. Justice is a bankbook," he said without bitterness. He stood up and set his empty glass on the table beside the sofa. "If that's it, we're about ready for dinner. Sorry we can't ask you to join us."

"That's all right," Bennett said. He finished his wine, rose, set his glass beside Thompson's, and walked to the door.

"There may be a couple of stories in the newspapers and on television about all of this," Bennett said. "Just ride them through. I doubt anyone'll bother you, however."

Thompson opened the door.

"Did you ever meet L. George Galley?" Bennett asked.

"A couple of times. Cool as a cucumber. Arrogant little bastard."

"How about his wife and son?" Bennett asked. "Did you know them?"

"He has a wife and son?" Thompson asked. "I'll be damned. Where's he keep them?"

"In La Jolla," Bennett replied. "His wife, anyway. There seems to be some confusion about where the son is." He looked at Thompson's strong, grave face. "Did you know that L. George Galley is dead? Died in a boating accident a couple of weeks ago. About the time you were attacked."

"No, I didn't know that. Good riddance," Thompson said.

Bennett thanked them both and left. He was going to find a phone so he could call the Great Northern hotel and see if Lester Galley was still there, but decided instead to stay in the northern part of the county and drive home on the Foothill Freeway. He didn't bother to call Polly and tell her he was on his way, because he assumed that by now she accepted his strange hours and abrupt comings and goings.

He stopped at a barbecue take-out on Ventura Boulevard and bought some ribs, in case she hadn't enough food prepared for the two of them. He drove into the garage, and as he entered the house called out: "I'm home. And don't worry about dinner, I bought some ribs."

She was sitting in the living room with a drink in her hand. She didn't greet him.

"Where'll I put the ribs?" he asked her.

"The kitchen would be a good place," she said, sipping her drink.

He knew the tone. He knew he was in trouble. He wrapped the ribs in foil and stuck them in a warm oven. Then he made himself a drink and walked back into the living room. He kissed the top of her head, the only surface she let him reach, and sat in the chair he usually occupied, a comfortable club chair that faced the television. It occurred to him as he sat down that he hadn't used it recently.

"How're you doing?" he asked her.

"Fine."

"Uh-huh. Well," he said, "I really got one hell of a lot of work done in La Jolla."

"Good for you."

"I know you think it was a waste of time, because of the chief announcing he'd caught the murderer. Well, believe me, Pol, it wasn't a waste of time. The chief's got the wrong man."

"He'll be delighted to hear that."

Bennett stared at her. "You mad at me?" he asked.

"No. I'm way past being mad at you. I've been mad

at you, I've been worried sick about you, I've been all sorts of things about you. Not any more."

"What? What'd you say?"

"I said not any more. We're done, Fred. I can't take it any longer. I spoke to a lawyer today."

He felt as though she'd hit him.

"What?" he said. "I don't understand. You spoke to a lawyer? About us?"

"That's right. He wanted me to change the locks on the doors. I told him that was uncivilized. He said to tell you you should probably get an attorney."

"What for?"

"I told you," she explained. "It's over. I can't take it any more."

"But I'm really on to something," he said desperately. "I mean, the things I found out in La Jolla are really going to break this case wide open. Wait'll you hear about it. I can't tell you now, of course, because I'm not quite finished. But this thing's not at all what it seemed to be. This will make every newspaper and wire service and TV evening news show. The chief's going to fall down when he hears what I've done, what I've come up with. Then the minute that's wrapped up, we're going to do some serious thinking about our future, just like I said. There's a whole big world out there, Pol, waiting for you and me."

She shook her head in disbelief. "Didn't you hear me?" she asked him. There was a brittle edge to her voice. She was getting angry, even though she had steeled herself for this. She had imagined the scene half a dozen times, during the last months when she was certain the break would have to be made, and she was the one who would have to make it. "It's no good going on," she said. "We've tried that. It's not working. Look at how you just reacted, when I told you I'd seen

233

a lawyer. You described what you'd been doing in La Jolla on the damn case. It's always some damn case! It's never us, what we're going to do! Well, no more! Not any damn more!"

He knew there was nothing he could say that would mollify her, so he sat quietly and drank his drink. Then he went into the garage and grabbed a couple of suitcases. He carried them into the bedroom and stuffed them with the clothes he guessed he would need until all this blew over, because he continued to hope it would. He believed that once the case was settled, once he was proved right and Drang and the chief wrong, then he would be able to speak to Polly about the future, and what they would do with their lives, and she would listen. Why, once the case was solved and he was proved right, there was no limit to what he would be able to do, and Polly would see that at once and be happy as hell to repair their damaged marriage.

"I'll stay in a motel until we get everything straightened out," he told her from the door. "And don't forget there are ribs in the oven."

She was going to call him back but she didn't. She had made her decision, and now she wanted a chance to see if she had made the right one. She heard him start his car and back out of the garage, and then she heard the garage door swing shut, and she let him go.

19

By the time he found a motel, Bennett had convinced himself that the scene with Polly was an aberration. He loved her and she loved him and they were married and it would all work out as soon as he wrapped up the case. He had chosen a motel in the valley where there was a restaurant just across the street. He checked into a small, neat room, then crossed the busy thoroughfare and had a drink and something to eat. He was so busy recalling the conversation he had had in La Jolla that when he finished the evening special, which was chicken pot pie, he asked to see a menu so that he could order dinner. The waitress decided he was some sort of smart ass.

"That's what you just ate, sir," she said plaintively, wondering if he was a harbinger of the loonies she should expect at her station that night.

"What?" Bennett was startled. Then he saw the bus boy taking away his plate. "Oh, hey, I'm sorry," he said, feeling like an idiot. "I was thinking of something else."

"I'll tell the chef how much you enjoyed your meal," she told him, escaping to the kitchen.

Bennett paid his check and crossed the street to the

motel room. In the phone book he found the number for the Great Northern Hotel. It was in the downtown area, in the central city, but not on skid row. A tired man's voice answered on the third ring, and Bennett asked to speak to Lester Galley. After a moment, the voice came back on the line.

"Who was that?" the voice asked.

"Lester Galley."

"No," the voice said. "There's no Lester Galley."

"He was there," Bennett said. "Did he leave a forwarding address?"

"He might have," the voice conceded.

"Would you look for me?" Bennett asked.

"That's not my department," the voice said. "If you're interested in knowing the forwarding address of one of our guests who used to stay here, then you'll have to come by in person, during business hours."

The voice didn't wait for Bennett's reply. The voice hung up the phone, and so did Bennett.

Lew Miller was his next call. He found Paramount Studios' night number, rang it, and when a Security Guard answered, said he was a relative of Lew Miller's and had to reach him before morning. The guard gave him Miller's home phone number and Bennett called it.

Miller answered the phone, and behind him a crowd cheered lustily. Bennett apologized for calling him at home.

"That's all right," Miller assured him. "I'm sitting here watching fights I've already seen. It's like I choreographed them by now. I know every step the bums take, every move."

"Why watch?" Bennett asked reasonably.

"It's better than talking to the old lady or the kids," Miller said. "Hang on a minute."

The sound level was considerably lowered.

"There, that's better," Miller said. "What's up? You get your masks?"

"No, not yet," Bennett said. "Listen, I understand L. George had a son."

"Oh yeah. Lester was the little bastard's name."

"Was he around when you were shooting 'Dungeons'?" Bennett asked.

"Well, let me see, when we were shooting 'Dungeons' Lester must have been only about four, five years old."

"Was he around when those masks were being used?" Bennett asked.

"Well, I had them in my prop room for the whole picture, it was such a made-up show I had to have them there in case somebody all of a sudden got a terrific idea to have everybody wear those damn masks. Even that little kid," he said. "A couple of times L. George made the little kid wear a mask."

"Why would he do that?"

"I don't know. Because it scared the hell out that kid, I suppose. Terrified the little bastard."

"You have any idea where Lester is these days?" Bennett asked.

"Hell, I haven't heard about him in years. Why?" Miller asked.

"Maybe he had some idea of what happened to those masks," Bennett lied.

"I told you L. George sold the whole lot of them."

"To Charlie Oliver, you said."

"That's right. To Charlie Oliver. How would Lester know where the hell they'd gone to, if his old man sold them to Charlie Oliver?" Miller asked.

"Yeah, right. Well, thanks for talking to me, and sorry to bother you at home," Bennett said. "Oh by the way, I don't think I gave you the number of the motel

237

where I'm staying. In case you hear anything, I'll probably be in town a couple of more days, maybe till the end of the week."

Bennett gave him the motel number and said goodnight. He turned on the television and got ready for bed. He punched channels until Chief Victor appeared on the screen, looking very sure of himself, a definite chief-of-police presence, although he'd had the class not to wear a full-dress uniform. The chief was talking about efficiency and certain established procedures, and how police work is not a matter for instinctive solutions. Good police work depends on a nuts-and-bolts approach to a crime, the chief said. You question witnesses, you examine evidence, you follow leads, you stake out buildings, you use the lab, you feed material to computers, and when you've triangulated this mountain of evidentiary material, good police work will point to the final step, which is the apprehension and arrest of the criminal. A case in point, the chief confided to a newscaster and the television audience, was the recent arrest of the man who allegedly murdered those poor souls down in the skid-row area of the city. He said allegedly, the chief continued, in order to protect the rights of the man who had confessed to the crimes. Justice is thus served, the chief pontificated, by way of good sound police work.

Bennett said "Bullshit" and changed to an old movie, which had something to do with a woman who was the head of a very large company and had an office as big as San Diego, out of the windows of which could be seen many other company buildings, writ on them in great letters several stories tall, the company's proud name, MILKRET. Bennett didn't turn the set off, although he was tired, because he wanted to find out what Milkret meant.

He fell asleep in the chair, and when he woke he thought for a moment he had the answer. On the screen a white-haired woman stood before a blackboard on which she was writing something in a very positive manner. It took Bennett a moment to realize she wasn't writing Milkret, this was a classroom in another picture, and she was teaching English to what looked like space urchins. He flicked off the set, turned out the lights, and went back to sleep.

He dreamed he was being chased through a Vietnamese jungle by a man covered with seaweed and dripping great rivers of water. Ever since he'd married Polly, she would awaken him when he began thrashing about in the bed in such nightmares, and her comforting presence would help him shake it off and return to a dreamless slumber. When he was away from her he had only himself to rely upon. He could awaken if he wished to, but the figure that chased him was covered with seaweed, and Bennett wanted to see the person's face before the dream ended. In this condition of being asleep yet beginning to be awake, his heart pounded and he broke out in a torrential night sweat. The figure drew closer still, until it was about to catch him. And then the mouth opened and the figure laughed. A great, jolly, rolling laugh. Bennett couldn't see the features, only a seaweed-covered head and an open mouth, laughing. Great howls of laughter.

They were so loud he awakened. Pale light leaked through the drawn blinds of his motel room. Outside he heard a trash truck, and along with it, a man's rollicking laughter. He heard a voice yell "Shut up," and when the laughter continued, someone bellowed irately "God damn it, shut up, don't you know people are still sleeping?"

By then everyone in the neighborhood must have

239

been awake. Bennett lay still, aware of his clammy body and pounding heart, until he recalled where he was and how he had gotten there and what he had been dreaming. Then he wearily slid out of bed and showered, shaved, and dressed. He combed his unruly black hair and stared into the mirror at his face, black eyes slack with fatigue, mouth unsmiling, and wondered if Polly was right, if he shouldn't be in some other work, where he could spend more time with her, raise a family, perhaps, which is what J. D. wanted him to do, and generally live a more normal life than he was able to do now.

He made instant coffee from a small packet of the stuff he mixed with water boiled in a miniature Silex, and drank it out of a yellow plastic cup provided by the management. He'd drunk half of it when the notion struck him.

As he drove away from the motel, he was aware that a black pickup was following him. He looked into his rearview mirror to see if he could identify the driver, but the sun reflected off the windshield, and he wasn't able to see who was in the car. This was not the first time he had seen it. When he left La Jolla he had seen a truck that might have been the same one, also going to Los Angeles, so he had not paid any attention to it; it was another in a stream of cars heading north. He had not looked for it outside Salvatore Thompson's house, but it might have been there. He certainly had not noticed if it had followed him home, and then to the motel. But it might have, he realized, because it was definitely tailing him now.

As he approached the Paramount auto gate, the pickup slowed, waiting to see what he was going to do. He stopped at the gate and greeted the guard, who remembered him from the day before and waved him through when he said he had some things to drop off at Lew Miller's office in the prop department. The black pickup remained outside the gates. When Bennett looked in his rearview mirror, he saw it turning around, ready to tail him again when he left.

Lew Miller was in his office, now empty of guns and ammunition.

"Hey, how goes it?" Miller greeted him. "You're a busy one, hm? Work work work."

"Well, hell, Lew," Bennett said, "you know better than me how much time it takes to get a show on the road."

"Do I," Miller said sadly.

"Listen, I meant to ask you," Bennett said. "L. George lives here in town, doesn't he?" He stopped himself. "I should say didn't he, I suppose."

"Yeah, he lived in Beverly," Miller said. "I think his wife had money. Somebody had money. You can't live L. George's life without having a bank behind you."

"You mean the women?" Bennett asked.

Miller looked at him. "Right. The women. L. George was a devil with the ladies. I think his wife finally went down to their place in La Jolla and settled in. She had the money, I heard. Her family. L. George stayed at the Beverly Hills house with Sonny."

"Sonny?"

"His kid. Lester. He always called him Sonny." He scratched the top of his head. "Now why in hell didn't I find a nice rich lady to marry so I could get the hell out of here?" He sighed. "Shit."

"Hang on a minute," Bennett said. He dashed out to his car and grabbed the film photo envelope he had been carrying around. Inside the office, he showed the picture to Lew Miller.

"Where'd you get this?" Lew Miller said.

"Is that L. George?" Bennett asked.

"That's him," Miller said, holding the picture as though it was a live memory. "That's L. George Galley, boy producer."

"His kid, Lester. You said he used to hang around with his daddy, come to the studio?"

"Right."

"Was this an unusual way for L. George to dress? All in black like that?"

"Hell, no. That was his outfit. Wore it every day."

"The boy saw his father wearing it?"

"Oh yeah. Of course. Like I say, L. George wore those clothes every day. Why?"

Instead of answering the question, Bennett said:

"You remember the address in Beverly where L. George lived? It's probably for sale, since he died. What the hell, maybe I could pick up a bargain."

"In Beverly Hills? That'll be the day." Miller opened an ancient address book. "Seven eleven Forrest," he said. "That's between Santa Monica and Sunset, and Forrest is a couple of blocks this side of Rexford."

"Thanks again," Bennett said.

When he drove out the gate he waved good-bye to the guard and mouthed see you soon. The black pickup waited until he had passed, and then pulled out after him. The driver wore a snow-white beard and dark glasses, so there was little of his face Bennett could see. Bennett made no effort to escape his tail. He politely waited at signals, and drove at a reasonable speed so that the white-bearded man wouldn't lose him in traffic. He turned north from Santa Monica onto Forrest, and parked in the seven-hundred block. The pickup passed him, and then, as if satisfied, drove to the next corner, turned around, and came back down the street. It slowed before it reached Bennett, turned

242

in to a driveway that bordered an enormous old house that resembled a Moroccan fortress, and disappeared behind the building. Bennett waited, then approached the great oak front door of seven-eleven Forrest and rang the bell. He had to ring a second time before anyone answered.

The door was opened by the white-bearded man who'd been driving the black pickup. He waited for Bennett to speak.

"Mr. Galley?" Bennett asked.

"Mr. Galley's dead," the white-beard said. "Two or three weeks ago."

"Oh I'm sorry to hear that," Bennett said.

"Um-hm," white-beard said noncommittally.

"How'd it happen?" Bennett asked.

"He drowned."

"Oh my goodness."

"Uh-hm."

Bennett had the feeling he was being studied from behind the dark glasses.

"You a friend of Mr. Galley's?" white-beard asked.

"From way back," Bennett said.

"Um-hm."

"How's the family taking it?" Bennett asked.

White-beard seemed surprised by the question. He moved back an inch or two. "You know the family?" he asked.

"Oh yeah. His wife and Lester both. How are they taking it?"

"As well as could be expected," white-beard said. "Have you known the family a long time?"

"Oh yeah."

"Um-hm."

"Are you taking care of the house?" Bennett asked.

"Why?"

"Well, with Mr. Galley gone, and his wife living in La Jolla, I figured someone had to watch out for this place and I wondered if you were the person in charge. Just curious."

"Uh-hm."

"Well, I'm sorry to hear about Mr. Galley. It seems like we always lose the best ones," Bennett said, and waited for another noncommittal sound.

White-beard didn't make any response. He stood there, eyeing Bennett from behind his heavy dark glasses.

"Wait'll I tell the others," Bennett said. "They'll be in shock."

"I'll bet," said white-beard. He didn't ask who the others were, he stepped back into the house and shut the door.

Bennett walked back to his car, slid in, and drove away. He stopped and parked at the next corner. Ten minutes later, the black pickup backed out of the driveway and headed for Santa Monica Boulevard. Bennett followed. The pickup pulled into a city parking lot close to Wilshire Boulevard. Bennett, keeping an eye on white-beard, parked in the adjoining lot. White-beard walked toward the Beverly Hills shopping district with Bennett behind him. He entered a real estate broker's office on Cañon, and Bennett waited across the street. In half an hour white-beard came out of the real estate office. He stood in the doorway talking to a tall slender man in well-cut clothes who smiled a great deal and reassuringly patted white-beard on the back. Then white-beard walked two doors down the street and entered a travel agency. Through the window, Bennett could see white-beard sit at a counter opposite a young black woman who produced schedules and maps and began writing something on a long sheet of paper. When she was finished, she showed white-beard what she had written. He studied it, asked a question, was satisfied with the reply, and pulled a wallet from his rear pocket. He handed the young woman some money. She counted it, then filled out several forms that might have been airline tickets. When she was done she gave them to white-beard. They shook hands, and he left the travel office. On the street he looked around, ignoring Bennett if he had seen him, and walked back to where he had parked the pickup. Bennett retrieved his car and followed white-beard to the house on Forrest. The pickup drove into the driveway and again disappeared. Bennett parked at the corner, facing the house.

And then Bennett saw the other car.

It was a blue Chevrolet, two doors, several years old, carrying California plates. Bennett noticed it because it circled the block. The first time it passed him he paid no attention. But then it came by a second time. He was waiting for it the third time. The driver wasn't interested in him; she paid no attention to him. Her eyes watched the house at seven-eleven. Bennett recognized her immediately.

The woman watching the Galley house was Franny Harris.

20

The blue Chevy circled the block a fourth time, then passed the Galley house and parked just beyond it. Franny Harris adjusted her rearview mirror so she could watch the front of the house and the driveway, and waited. Bennett wished he had a cup of coffee, but didn't move.

In Vietnam there had been long periods of waiting. Not ordinary army waiting, where a soldier is ordered to report at X hours to Y place at the command of Z officer, and there soldier stands, his life wasting away, until someone somewhere remembers why he's there and either gives him something aimless to do or dismisses him. The waiting periods Bennett remembered in Vietnam came when he was on patrol, on search and destroy, after they had reached a place in the jungle where Cong were suspected of operating. They would dig in, crouched down in the jungle, hardly daring to breathe, waiting, waiting for someone to shoot at them, or attack them, or bomb them, or come screaming out of the jungle at them. Waiting, hearts pounding so loudly it seemed the Cong would hear the sound. A young soldier close to Bennett, a replacement on his first s. and d., had become so frightened when there was a sudden rattle of rifle fire that he had peed in his pants and not realized it until the action was over with no casualties—if you didn't count being scared to death, or facing a life where a recurring nightmare would be the terrible memory of yourself in the jungle at night under attack from all sides by faceless, bodyless creatures you didn't know who wanted to maim and kill you.

The black pickup backed out of the driveway, several boxes lying on the bed. Bennett started his motor. It headed west at the cross-street below the house, the blue Chevy behind it. Bennett followed the blue Chevy. The three cars proceeded west until they had reached Sepulveda. There the black pickup stopped at a large warehouse building that fronted railroad tracks still in use for freight deliveries. White-beard got out and without looking at the cars that had been following him, entered the unidentified building. The blue Chevy passed the black pickup and stopped at the end of the building. Bennett stayed a block away.

He thought he saw something move in the back of the Chevy. He wondered if Franny Harris had a dog, and had brought it with her. A dog that had been lying on the seat or had lain down on the floor in the narrow space between the front and back seats. A black dog, it looked like.

Or a slight man, dressed all in black.

White-beard came out of the building followed by a man in work clothes pushing a dolly. When the man turned away from Bennett, "Westside Storage" could be seen stenciled on the back of his shirt. The man lifted the packages from the bed of the pickup and loaded them on the dolly, handed white-beard a sheet of paper, and wheeled his dolly back inside the building.

White-beard climbed into the pickup and started off. But he turned suddenly at the corner of the building and disappeared. The blue Chevy roared after him, with Bennett in pursuit. There was no sign of the pickup. The loading dock on this side of the building was empty. The Chevy stopped, and Franny Harris was about to get out when, in her rearview mirror, she saw Bennett's car behind her. She slammed her door and drove off. Whatever it was in the back seat slid down out of view.

Bennett parked. Through a large side door that opened into the building, he saw another door at the opposite end through which he guessed white-beard had escaped.

He drove back to Beverly Hills, to the real estate office where he had seen white-beard, and approached the tall, elegant man to whom white-beard had been talking. On the elegant man's desk was a brass nameplate reading "Mr. Serafian."

Bennett stood in front of the desk until Mr. Serafian looked up.

"I'm looking for a house," Bennett said. "Here in Beverly Hills would satisfy my heart's desire. Is there anything available?"

Mr. Serafian looked doubtfully at Bennett's inexpensive grey suit and scuffed shoes, but had the manners to gesture toward a chair which faced the desk.

"Won't you sit down," he said, in a voice that oozed disdain. "I'm Vargas Serafian." He held out a tanned well-manicured hand.

"Pleasure," Bennett said, taking the offered hand and shaking it crisply. "Fred Bennett."

"Oh yes," Serafian said, as though Bennett had just identified himself as one of the three richest men in the world. "Fred Bennett."

"The neighborhood that interests me lies north of Santa Monica and south of Sunset," Bennett explained. "As an example of a street I think has great beauty, I would say Forrest Drive."

Serafian's eyebrows jumped convulsively.

"Would something be available there?" Bennett asked.

"There might be," Serafian said, testing the water. "Forrest Drive, you said?"

Bennett admitted that Forrest Drive was what he had said.

"I believe we may have just today received the authority to sell a home in that area," Serafian said.

"Would that be the Galley home?" Bennett asked.

Serafian's eyebrows leaped once again.

"I'm aware of the terrible accident that caused Mr. Galley's death," Bennett explained. "That's why I presumed the Galley home might be for sale. Unless the probate . . . ?"

"No no no," Serafian said quickly. "Mr. Galley had made plans to sell the property before the unfortunate accident you've mentioned. We've only been awaiting the arrival of Mr. Galley's brother to bring us certain papers. . . ."

"Is Mr. Galley's brother a resident of this area?"

"I believe not," Serafian said. "But he did arrive with the necessary signed papers giving us the authority to act as agents in the sale of the property." He stopped, licked his lips, cleared his throat and stared at Bennett's tie, which, from the expression on Serafian's face, must have been stained just below the knot with fresh blood. "The property," he continued, "will be

249

listed as partially furnished. There is a swimming pool and there is room for a north-south tennis court. We are asking four million eight."

To Bennett's credit he didn't laugh aloud or say you must be kidding. He took the news calmly.

"If you have been looking for a Beverly Hills home," Serafian said easily, "you will understand what a bargain the Galley property is."

"No question about it," Bennett said. "How long has Mr. Galley's brother been in town?"

This surprised Serafian. "How long?" he asked, puzzled.

"I'm trying to figure out in my mind if the property has been sitting there unattended."

Serafian didn't let him finish. "No, no," he said, "it was never unattended. I understand your concern, but no no the property has never been unattended. Mr. Galley's brother arrived only yesterday, I believe, but the property has been attended since the owner's unfortunate accident, I assure you."

"Sometimes, in the face of such a tragedy . . ." Bennett said, waving his hands vaguely.

"I quite understand," Serafian said.

Bennett rose. "If I could have your card," he said. "I'll discuss this with my people, and get back to you."

"I'll set up an appointment for you to see the house whenever you desire. I would only have to call the housekeeper."

"Perfect," Bennett said, accepting the business card Serafian offered. "Thank you for your help."

He shook Serafian's hand once more, and left.

He drove to Westwood, and parked his car a few doors away from Franny Harris's home. The blue Chevy was in the driveway. Somber skies threatened rain, the first of the season. Bennett had never grown

250

used to Southern California's dryness, although he'd lived there most of his life, except for a few years just after his mother's death when J. D. had taken him to Las Vegas. There the two of them had lived in a suite on the top floor of one of the largest hotels. And it was there that Bennett had learned not to discuss money with his stepfather. The boy had innocently questioned J. D. about why they had no credit cards or charge accounts, about why all bills were paid in cash, never by check. J. D. sat young Bennett down and read him a stern but loving lecture on the subject of money. It was never to be discussed, he told the boy, and in fact if anyone were ever to ask Bennett anything at all about J. D.'s money, where it came from or what he did with it, Bennett was to tell the inquirer politely it wasn't any of their goddam business, and then he was to button his goddam lip. Bennett got the message.

Franny Harris stepped out of her house carrying two suitcases and a garment bag, which she laid in the trunk of the Chevy. She slammed the trunk shut and went back into the house. When she came out again she was wearing a hat and a coat and carrying a purse and a small makeup case. She double-locked her front door, got into the car, and started it, but instead of backing out into the street, she drove forward and disappeared behind the house. Bennett was about to pull up so he could see what she was doing when she reappeared. She backed slowly out of her driveway and drove away from Bennett, toward Beverly Glen. He followed her. She turned east on Wilshire, and once in the center of Beverly Hills, turned north on Crescent, parked opposite the post office, and walked quickly into the building. Bennett passed her car; a warm coat was lying on the back seat. He pulled up ahead of where she had stopped. Within five minutes she hurried out of the post office, shutting her purse. She got into her car but didn't drive away. She sat there. Bennett watched her in his rearview mirror. Her hat, a mannish round-crowned felt, framed her haughty face. She looked drawn as she stared straight ahead. She glanced at her wristwatch several times, and then, satisfied, started her car and drove off.

Bennett started his motor.

"Hold it, Fred."

Sean MacManus stood on the pavement, leaning in the passenger window of the car. Ahead, Franny Harris turned right on Santa Monica and disappeared in the traffic.

"I can't now, Sean," Bennett said to his fellow cop. He gestured toward the boulevard ahead. "Tailing someone."

"Drang wants to talk to you," Sean said. "He's really pissed off, Fred. What the hell did you do to make him so mad?"

"Listen, Sean . . ."

The young officer opened the door and got in beside Bennett. "He hasn't put an A. P. B. out for you because he said he didn't want to embarrass you and the chief and the department and all that shit. He got us together, the guys who worked with you on that slasher thing downtown, and he told us to keep our eyes open and if we saw you, to make sure you came along with us so he could talk to you. He's really pissed off, Fred," he repeated. His pale, freckled skin was flushed with excitement. "You know Drang," he said. "So I have to do what he tells me to do, right?"

"Yeah, sure," Bennett agreed, planning alternatives. "Where is Drang?"

"Downtown. But he said to call him if one of us

saw you. He doesn't want us to bring you into head-quarters."

"He doesn't want to embarrass me or the chief or the department," Bennett dryly echoed.

"You got it," MacManus said. "That's it exactly." He looked at Bennett almost shyly. "He's really pissed off," he said again, with wonder in his voice. "What the hell did you do? I thought the two of you were buddies."

"I told him he was wrong."

Sean didn't believe Bennett. Drang wouldn't get so furious he'd threaten to have Bennett drawn and quartered if he was ever seen again, just because Bennett had said Drang was wrong about something.

"I'm parked right behind you," Sean said. "I'll call in and see where you go to meet Drang." He looked at Bennett, his earnest blue eyes imploring. "Please don't try anything, Fred. I mean, this is a terrible spot I'm in, and I've got a lot invested in my work, you know? So just sit here until I come back. Okay?"

"Okay." Bennett turned off the motor.

Sean slid out of the car backwards. He hurried to his car, got in, and used his radio, never taking his eyes off Bennett.

"Drang was at his place," Sean reported, when he returned. "He said stay here. Then he laughed and said to tell you it'll be better to meet you here because this is neutral territory. Funny, huh?"

"Hysterical," Bennett said.

"And he said if I left you alone for a second, or if you got away, it was my ass." He looked beseechingly at Bennett.

"I'll wait for Drang," Bennett promised, wondering how long it would take, and whether he would be able

253

to get away from Drang and Sean before white-beard skipped town.

They waited ten minutes. When Drang arrived, he parked in front of Bennett, then backed up until their bumpers touched. Sean got out of the car and Drang slid in.

"When'd you get back?" he asked Bennett.

"Yesterday, I think."

"I told you to report in. You didn't. Why?"

"Let's not go around again, Drang," Bennett said. "It's really very tedious. You think you've caught a murderer, and I think you've made a mistake."

"Tedious?" Drang said. "This case is the chief's personal project. The murderer was picked up, the murderer has confessed."

"The murderer I'm looking for attacked a man in Pasadena," Bennett said. "Did your suspect confess to that?"

"Pasadena?" Drang repeated. "Impossible." He wavered, and Bennett recognized an opportunity.

"While we're talking," Bennett said, aware of the moving clock on his dashboard, "everything I've been working on is coming to a head. Now you know damn well it's not going to make a hell of a lot of difference to you one way or the other if I don't report in for another forty-eight hours. No difference at all. Am I right?"

Drang grudgingly admitted that Bennett was right.

"Here's your bottom line," Bennett said. "If I'm right, the chief can announce that he suspected the confession all along, and used it as a tactic to force the hand of the real murderer. He can say he feels an adjunct of good police work is to make certain that those poor sick folks who confess to crimes have medical attention to ease their guilts. He can point out that the media used that sick confession to sell newspapers and increase TV ratings. Jesus, there's a million things he could say."

Drang looked doubtful.

"I swear to you that if I haven't resolved my investigation within forty-eight hours I'll turn everything I have over to you, and you can do whatever you want with it. If you think I'm barking up the wrong tree, forget it. Now that's pretty damn fair." Bennett was perspiring. He knew he was right and he needed time to prove it. He also knew that Drang might have had a bellyful of stories and might now be unwilling to listen to anything more. They had a man, the man had confessed, they could neatly wrap up everything and accept congratulations. Case complete. Close the file. Solved. Applause for Chief Victor. Have you thought of running for public office, chief? After much shit-kicking, well, yes, some supporters have brought up the subject. But my duty is to the department. My duty is to make this the finest police department in the country. In the world. But if you were asked, would you run for mayor? For governor? For senator? For president? Well, my supporters have mentioned my running for public office, but my duties . . .

"All right," Drang said. "Forty-eight hours. Here are the conditions. First: if, after forty-eight hours, you have nothing more than what you have now, that's the end of it, as far as your case is concerned. Second: if, during the forty-eight-hour period you come up with something that's contrary to what we already have, you turn it over to us and you keep your mouth shut. It's important to the chief that he wind this thing up, be in at the finish, since he's been on top of it since the beginning. Agreed?"

Bennett thought about it only for an instant. He wanted to solve the case so badly he would have agreed to anything.

So he agreed to abide by Drang's conditions. He made a promise it would be impossible for him to keep.

21

Bennett had been waiting outside the Galley house for nearly three hours. He knew white-beard was inside; he had seen him moving around. He didn't know what had become of Franny Harris since she'd driven away from the post office. Although he had moved his car several times, a gardener and a citizen in a jogging suit had looked at him suspiciously, but Bennett had flashed his friendliest smile and they had doubtfully accepted his presence. Children had come home from school, the younger ones walking or riding ten-speed bicycles, the teen-agers driving high-powered cars they gunned noisily as they pulled into their driveways. Because of the overcast skies, evening came earlier and corner street-lamps lighted and dropped yellow pools on scrubbed sidewalks. Beverly Hills was a community like any other, Bennett decided, except there was more of everything. Bigger homes, greener lawns, more perfectly colored gardens and more expensive cars. (Six Rolls-Royces had driven by in the three hours Bennett had been waiting.) The only fault he could find was that these million-dollar homes nearly touched, your kitchen was only half a dozen feet from my maid's privy. If it was privacy you wanted, you had it only in front and in back.

Lights were turned on in the Galley house, and Bennett could see white-beard moving through the front room, stopping at tables, at bookcases, making his last farewells to his late brother's belongings. Good-bye books, good-bye paintings, good-bye grand piano, good-bye, good-bye, good-bye. Then the lights in the room were turned off. One by one, in other rooms, lights flashed on, remained lit long enough for white-beard to make his farewells, and then, except for two dim lamps, the house was dark.

Half an hour later, when no evidence of day could be seen in the western sky, Bennett heard a car motor start up. After a moment a Cadillac Eldorado backed out of the drive and onto Forrest. White-beard sat behind the wheel, and it seemed to Bennett that he looked pleased about something.

The Cadillac headed south, Bennett a block behind. When Bennett had driven a block from the Galley house, a third car, which had been parked at the corner north of the house, followed the others. Bennett, intent on keeping white-beard in sight, was unaware that he was also being followed. The Cadillac led the way along quiet residential streets, following a route that would take them to the airport.

They were in the Culver City area, approaching the San Diego freeway, when the third car disappeared. And two blocks later it happened. Without warning the third car sped out of a cross-street and struck the Cadillac. It was a superficial accident—Bennett, a block behind, could see it but barely hear it. But it stopped the Cadillac. Then, suddenly, the passenger door of the third car opened and a figure leaped out and jumped into the front seat of the Cadillac beside the driver. There was a flurry of indistinguishable movement, then the figure hurried back to the third car, which had backed off from the collision, hopped back in, and the car raced away from the accident scene, tires squealing. All this happened before Bennett could get there. By the time he arrived, the third car had disappeared.

Bennett stopped and hurried to the Cadillac. White-beard clutched the wheel with both hands. The beard, no longer white, was streaked with crimson as blood gushed from the horrible wound in his neck.

"Oh God!" white-beard said, his voice drowning. "Oh Jesus!" He tried to breathe, tried desperately to hold his throat together, his hands grasping at the wound, as if that would prevent his life from escaping in surging, rushing blood.

Bennett used his car radio to call for help, then returned to the dying man.

White-beard's blue eyes were dull, his face was growing slack. "How could he do it?" he whispered. "Bastard."

"Did you recognize him?" Bennett asked.

"Bastard," white-beard repeated, the word slipping out of his mouth. "Missed last time."

"Do you know who did it?" Bennett repeated urgently. "Was it Sonny?"

"Mask," white-beard said. "Little bastard."

"A porcelain mask?" Bennett asked.

The head was too heavy to be supported, and it fell forward, causing blood to spurt. White-beard's hands, in a final agony, gripped the steering wheel and sounded the horn. An ear-splitting warning blew, continued blowing, until Bennett reached into the car and tore the hands from the horn rim. In the distance he heard an approaching siren. There was nothing more he could do for the dying man. He hurried to his car and left the scene before ambulance and police arrived.

He used his radio as he drove, and was able to reach Drang without identifying himself.

"You're in for a surprise," he said. "If you dig resurrections."

"What's that mean?" Drang asked.

"A dead man is alive and then dead."

He told Drang that ambulance and black and white were at the scene, and ended the conversation.

He drove north, hands clammy against the wheel until he realized they were bloody. He found an open gas station and parked beside the washrooms. A startled attendant cautiously watched him enter the men's room, and was still standing there, alert, waiting for disaster, when Bennett came out, hands clean, got back into his car, and sped away.

He drove back to Paramount, explained to a new guard, a heavy-set woman working the four-to-twelve shift, that he had a meeting with Lew Miller in the Prop Department. She wasn't one to be fooled by black-haired men with black glittering eyes, and she called before letting Bennett through. Miller must have said it was all right, because when she hung up the phone she raised the gate and said "You know where it is?" Bennett assured her that he did, thanked her for her courtesy, and drove onto the lot. He parked where he had on each of his previous trips and was surprised to see that two stages were still in use, flashing red lights at the heavy doors warning people not to enter while cameras were rolling.

Lew Miller was sitting behind his desk with his feet on a stack of packing cases. He had a fine cut-glass water goblet in his hand, and had placed another on the desk beside a matching decanter filled with amber liquid.

"We are going to celebrate the end of the day," Miller said. "Scotch whiskey. Help yourself."

Bennett did, pouring a double shot into his glass.

"You will note that when the picture that's shooting calls for the best in cut glass we are set up to supply it. If we were making a Western, we'd be drinking out of cheap shot glasses. Around here we live the life of the picture that's shooting." He waved to a chair opposite the desk and Bennett sat down.

"To hard work," Lew Miller said, holding up his glass. Bennett raised his, and they both drank. "What's up?" Lew Miller asked.

"You told me you knew Franny Harris," Bennett said.

"Yeah, I knew Franny."

"When?"

Lew Miller slid his feet off the packing case. His chair creaked as he swung it around so that he faced his desk.

"Fred Bennett," he said. "Is that really your name?"

Bennett blinked. "That's my name," he said. "Why?"

"I have some friends in Chicago. You're not in the phone book. They're in the entertainment business. They never heard of you."

"Maybe we just never ran across each other," Bennett explained.

"I also have some friends here in L.A.," Miller said. "These L.A. friends, they're familiar with a lot of people on the police department. One of these friends told me there's a cop on the L.A.P.D. whose name is Fred Bennett. Would that be you?"

Bennett weighed his options very quickly. "That's a reasonable assumption," he said.

Lew Miller stared at him. "Why the hell don't you guys come and tell people who you are and what you're up to?"

"Most of the time we do," Bennett said. "In this case I couldn't."

Miller nodded. "I should have known because even though you don't look like a cop, you ask questions like one. You don't sound like a movie producer, you sound like a cop."

"Next time I'll be more careful," Bennett said.

"Franny Harris, you asked me," Lew Miller said. "Did I know her. Yes, I did."

"When?" Bennett asked.

"When she was a script girl. She was one gorgeous thing, let me tell you. Tall, elegant, something else. And a hell of a script girl."

"Was she on 'Dungeons'?"

"Let's see, somewhere in there, she got a better offer, to be Charlie Oliver's executive secretary, and she took the job." He pressed his fingers to his forehead. "What the hell am I talking about? Of course she was on 'Dungeons.' I remember how she and the kid used to get along so great."

"The kid?"

"Sonny. Lester. L. George's kid. Him and Franny were real pals. I remember that kid was crazy about Franny. He had a real crush on her. He'd do any damn thing she asked him to." He sipped more of his drink. "Yeah," he said. "Franny Harris was on 'Dungeons.' She was the script girl on the show. She didn't go to work for Charlie Oliver until after we finished the picture."

262

"So she knew Sonny, and she knew about the masks, 'way back then," Bennett said.

"Yeah, right," Lew Miller agreed, "Franny Harris knew L. George's kid and she knew about the masks 'way back then."

22

Bennett heard it on the car radio as he drove off the Paramount lot: another slashing murder; this time the victim had been driving a car, an expensive car. There'd been an accident, a hit-and-run accident because the second car had driven off, according to neighbors who'd heard the racket, and the killer must have been passing by, looking for a victim, and he'd seen a disabled man in the expensive car and he'd struck. Chief Victor admitted this crime cast doubts on the validity of the confession of the suspect already in custody, but promised the media the department was on top of the case and would have an announcement within hours regarding this new turn of events. Also, the radio newsman continued, the chief confirmed a report that the police internal investigative board was pursuing a case in which an officer had been accused of taking bribes and pocketing department money. There was a great deal of evidence against the officer, the chief said, but further investigation was in progress—which was, of course, within the purview of the department, he concluded, in what sounded like doublespeak.

Bennett felt the skin crawl on the back of his neck.

He turned off the radio. *Well,* he thought, *Drang warned me I'd get my balls cut off if I kept at it.*

He drove through the east gate and up the curving two-lane road. He parked opposite the house and walked quietly across the street. Lights were on in the downstairs rooms, and upstairs in a bedroom a lamp softly glowed. The driveway curved past the front door where it divided, one tentacle reaching back to the street, the other winding between oleanders to the rear of the house, where twin garages faced each other across a used-brick courtyard, giving the impression that the buildings were in the French countryside and not Los Angeles, California. Bennett followed the winding drive to the rear. He stopped when he saw the Chevy, parked in a shadow. He approached it cautiously. The right front headlight was broken and the fender bent. Bennett wanted to look inside for bloodstains, but the car was locked. He hurried back to the front door and rang the bell. In a moment the door opened, and Charlie Oliver stood there, wearing baggy pants and a UCLA sweatshirt that had "Go Bruins" stenciled on it.

"Well," Oliver said when he saw Bennett. "They work on movies this late in Chicago?"

"Could I come in?" Bennett asked. "I've run into a couple of problems."

"Sure, sure," Charlie Oliver said, stepping back so Bennett could enter the house. "I like it when a guy is so hot about business he forgets the time. That's the sort of concentration got me this nice little house."

The heavy door closed with a solid, rich thump behind Bennett, and then Charlie Oliver scooted ahead. "Living room all right?" he asked. "Some people think a living room is a place for formality. Me, I consider it to be just what its name implies: a room in which you

265

live. Come in, come in. Sit yourself down. How about a drink? Coffee or tea or milk or booze or beer or what? What would you care for?"

Bennett thanked his host, declined anything to drink, and sat down in a great club chair, swinging his legs onto a matching ottoman. Charlie Oliver stood in front of the fireplace under the painting of a beautiful woman, a full-length portrait done in the manner of Gainsborough.

"My daughter Gwen," he told Bennett. "Painted just before her marriage. Did you ever see anything so ravishingly beautiful? Eileen takes after her mother. Eileen's gone to bed," he said. "She'll be sorry she missed you."

The old man seemed to be high on something. He was talkative, bright, assured, pleased, full of high spirits. He stood below the portrait of his daughter and rocked back and forth on the balls of his feet. He rubbed his hands together.

"You act like a man who's had good news," Bennett observed. "Your ship come in?"

Charlie Oliver grinned. "Naw," he said. "Just pleased to be alive and well. When you get to be my age there's a lot fewer ships, and a lot less frequent arrivals. Now when I was a young man, I had ships sailing all the seven seas, to use your metaphor, so each day there was the chance one of them might come in. Or might not," he added with a wicked grin. "One of them might sink. Might settle to the bottom of whatever sea it was on, never to be heard from again." His gaze strayed back to the portrait. "Well," he said, "here I am philosophizing all over the place and you're patiently listening to me when you've got more important things on your mind than whether or not Charlie Oliver's got ships still sailing the seas. You've run into a couple of problems, I believe you said. Well, I'm at your disposal."

"I think I've located those masks," Bennett said.

"Well good; good for you. Sorry I couldn't have been of more help to you there." Charlie Oliver smiled. He was friendly and open.

"I was trying to remember," Bennett said. "When was it you bought them?"

"Gosh," Oliver said, "I'd have to look that up. I don't have the date right here at the tip of my fingers."

"Would it have been right after Gwen's death?" Bennett asked.

Charlie Oliver stopped smiling. "Well, I don't really know." He looked at Bennett. "Is that information you need, now that you've located the masks?"

"I think it was right after Gwen's death," Bennett said. "I think you were bereft, and you bought those masks. Incidentally," he continued, "how'd you know about them?"

"I don't recall what brought it to my attention," Charlie Oliver said. "Could have been almost anything, any of a hundred different things. I might have suddenly remembered the picture—what the devil was it called? 'The Dungeons of Hell County'? I might have remembered the picture and thought the masks were something I could use in this film I was planning. . . ."

"The one you stopped work on when you got ill?" Bennett asked.

"Yes. Exactly." Charlie Oliver looked at Bennett more carefully. "I'm not sure I understand how all this has anything to do with this documentary-type thing you're doing in Chicago," he said.

"Is it possible you heard about the masks from Franny Harris?" Bennett asked quietly.

"Ahhhh," Charlie Oliver said in a breath. "Let's see." He frowned and touched his hand to his forehead. "I'm thinking," he explained. "I'm thinking." He held the position for a few moments. An old man in baggy pants wearing a UCLA sweatshirt with "Go Bruins" stenciled on it, skinny right hand to bony forehead. "Do you want to know what I'm thinking?" he asked Bennett.

Bennett didn't reply. He waited for Oliver to continue.

"I'm thinking that you're probably not what you've made yourself out to be." He lowered his hand. "I'm thinking that you're not in the motion-picture business, and possibly not from Chicago. Am I warm?" he asked.

"That's a possibility," Bennett admitted.

"There's ways I can check," Charlie Oliver said. Then: "You should know that this house, all this property around here, is patrolled. There've been a couple of robberies, and so these houses around here are wired. There's all sorts of communications can be put to work, just at the flick of a switch. We're more careful here than down at La Jolla. For example, I recall an attempted robbery happened a couple of months ago—I don't know if you read about it in the papers—some bastard tried to break into one of the houses around here and an alarm was tripped and before you could say 'Jack Robinson' patrol cars were here and this would-be burglar found himself in a very serious and precarious position. To make a long story short this would-be burglar made the wrong move and he was shot. Killed, as a matter of fact, because it appeared to the patrolling officer who got the alarm and rushed over, it seemed to that officer that this man I'm talking about was reaching for a weapon." He wiped

268

his mouth with the back of his hand. Spittle had appeared at the corner of his lips, and he wiped it away. "You carrying a gun?" he asked. "Because if you are you're in one hell of a lot of trouble. Take my word for it. This area of the city shoots first and asks questions afterwards."

"Where's Franny Harris?"

"Why ask me?"

"Her car's in the back."

Oliver shook his head. He might have been saying he had no explanation for why Franny Harris's car was in the back of his house, or he might have been wondering how Bennett had gotten to be such an idiot.

"Is Sonny here too?" Bennett asked. "What are you going to do with him now? Cast him adrift? Let him run loose? You're finished with the little bastard. You've got your revenge."

Charlie Oliver's face was scarlet. His lips trembled. "Who in hell are you?" he asked, his voice rasping.

"I'll tell you who he is," someone said from the doorway.

Bennett turned his head. Sonny stood at the living room entrance, a butcher knife in his hand: slackly held, so that it might have been anything, a golf club, an umbrella, anything but the glittering razor-sharp instrument of death it was.

"When I saw him downtown, before," Sonny continued, "I had a strong feeling about him. What I think he is, is a cop. I thought so then; now I know so." He took a few steps into the room. "You're in one hell of a spot, cop," he said. "You're breathing your last, because one more don't make the slightest difference to me. One more or a dozen more. I paid back who I wanted to pay back, now one or two more, what the hell, it doesn't mean any more than the first ones.

You're discards, all of you. Fucking discards. Left-overs. Throwaways."

"Take it easy," Oliver cautioned.

"Oh yeah, sure, take it easy," Sonny said. There were blood stains on his black clothing, dark stains where his bloodied hands had touched his trousers and his sweater. "You want me to put on the mask?" he asked Bennett. "Then you won't even know what happened. The last thing you'll see is that pretty face looking at you." He moved two steps closer.

Franny Harris had entered the room. "Charlie?" she said, her voice shaking.

"It's all right," Oliver replied. "It's all right. We can take care of it. Nothing to worry about."

She walked into the room, stepped past Sonny and his knife, and stood beside Charlie Oliver. "Is Eileen asleep?" she asked.

"Yes," he said. "But go upstairs and stay with her until we're finished here."

She obediently left the room, and Bennett could hear her hurrying upstairs.

"She always do exactly what you tell her to?" Bennett asked Charlie Oliver.

"Always. She's very efficient." Charlie Oliver allowed himself a tight smile. "I can only work with someone who's the best there is at their particular job."

"Like Sonny?"

"Like Sonny. Yes. Sonny's an expert. Aren't you, Sonny?"

"You bet your ass," Sonny said. He raised the knife and tested the blade against his thumb. "When I was a kid my father told me, I don't care what you do, just be the best at it. He's pleased as hell, don't you think?" he asked Bennett.

Bennett started to move in the chair. Sonny pointed

270

the knife, casually, as if it was an extension of his hand.

"Prick," Sonny said, "that's what my old man was. A prick." He turned to Charlie Oliver. "You should've seen his face when he saw me. He got one look at the clothes and the mask and he says, 'Oh my God, oh my God.' You should've seen the expression on his face." Once again, he drew the knife blade across his thumb. It cut slightly, and he held up the injured hand, thumb down, and watched a drop of blood form, hang suspended, then drop to the carpet.

"Did Mr. Oliver tell you who it was you attacked in Pasadena?" Bennett asked. Charlie Oliver looked surprised.

"Why should he tell me?" Sonny asked. "What the hell difference? He pointed the man out to me. 'There's one,' he says. 'Dazzle 'em,' he says to me." He gestured toward Oliver with the knife. " 'It's all show biz,' he says to me. 'One here, one there, build yourself a little reputation, get everybody dazzled, confuse them, then lower the boom, they'll never know who did it.' " He shook his head in admiration. "Oh man, what good advice that was." He nearly smiled, lips tightly drawn back but closed, no perfect white teeth exposed. "It's like the recording I sent to the radio station," he said. "Did you hear it? He wrote it, and I recited the damn thing. Good, you know? Classy. Razzle-dazzle. Confuse them. You ever hear it?"

"I heard it," Bennett said quietly. Sonny nodded his head rapidly. "Did you know the man who confessed to the murders?" Bennett asked.

"Oh yeah. I told him to," Sonny bragged. "This sonofabitch was complaining no one knew who he was. This poor sonofabitch said he could disappear from the face of the fucking earth and no one would miss him because they didn't know he'd been here. You know what I said to him?" He didn't wait for a reply. "I said to him, 'I'll tell you how to get people to pay attention to you and know you're alive. Confess to those murders.' Crazy sonofabitch bought it. I told him a couple of things to say and he said them and made a big confession and the cops believed him. Stupid bastards."

"They'll have to let him off now," Bennett said.

"Why? You think you'll tell them? No. You're going to die. But I'll do you differently, so it's not like the ones he confessed to. There's more than one fucking way to skin a cat," he said, threatening with the knife. "Maybe I'll skin you."

Charlie Oliver licked his lips and wiped sweating hands over the words "Go Bruins." "Take it easy, Sonny," he said.

"Why'd your father fake that accident?" Bennett asked, trying to keep Sonny talking.

"Because he knew I was going to kill him." Sonny nearly laughed once again, the tightly closed lips grotesquely pulled back. "I jumped him one night. He got a look at that mask and this outfit and he shit. I was going to finish him then but he was so scared I thought, I'll let him be scared for a while, like I always was when I was a kid. I'll let him sweat for a while about when I'm finally going to get him. So the prick made believe he drowned. I knew he didn't drown. That prick could swim with a rock tied to his back. Swimming is something he can do nearly as good as fuck all those chicks and make my mother yell and scream and cry. So I knew he didn't die. I brought the box of masks to his house so he'd understand I knew he wasn't dead. He'd know I was still after him. All he didn't know was when I'd do it. Hey? I got him good, right? He didn't think that's where it would happen."

He rubbed the hand that held the knife across his upper lip, where dots of perspiration had appeared. "You should've seen him," he marveled. "Oh, man." The memory suffused his face, softening his angry eyes.

"You've done enough talking," Charlie Oliver said.

"What?" Sonny asked. He was startled to be dragged out of his reverie. "What'd you say? I'd done enough talking?"

"Shut up," Oliver said.

"No, no, no," Sonny said. "You've got it all wrong. I shut up when I want to shut up. I speak when I want to speak."

Bennett was helpless in the big chair, his feet on the ottoman. He had to get up and make things happen his way, not sit in a damn club chair with his feet up on a giant ottoman while a madman with a knife stood above him. He made a single dangerous move. He leaped to his feet with a yell.

"What're you doing?" Sonny screamed. "What the hell do you think you're doing?" He raised the knife, prepared to attack.

"I had a charley-horse," Bennett said. "Take it easy, for God's sake, I had a charley-horse. Why would I jump up when you're the one with the knife? You're in control, Sonny. You know that."

"Damn right," Sonny said, lowering the knife.

Bennett stood in a clear space, with Charlie Oliver on his right and Sonny directly ahead. The living-room door was to his left, in his line of sight if Franny Harris or anyone else came in. "You've been in control all along, Sonny. Did you know he claims he set you up to do this?" He gestured his thumb toward Charlie Oliver. "You want to know what he told me? He told me he wanted revenge on your old man because your old man killed his daughter."

273

"I told you nothing," Charlie Oliver yelled.

"You wanted revenge," Bennett said. "You bought those masks right after Gwen killed herself. . . ."

"She didn't kill herself. She would never do that. She was murdered. By his father." Charlie Oliver stared up at the portrait. "He murdered her," he said.

"Franny knew about the masks," Bennett said. "And she knew Sonny. Efficient Franny figured out how to do two things at the same time. You'd get your revenge, and Sonny would get even with his father."

"You should have seen his face," Sonny agreed. "When he saw that mask and the outfit and the knife, you should have seen his goddam face. He crapped, I'll bet you. I bet he shit in his pants." Sonny looked over at Charlie. "I did what you said," he told him. "Just before I did it I said to him, 'Charlie Oliver asks to be remembered.'"

Sonny was facing Charlie Oliver. Bennett acted quickly. His shoe cracked Sonny's wrist and the knife fell to the carpet. As Sonny bent to pick it up, Bennett kicked hard at Sonny's exposed chin. The little man fell to the floor without a sound. Bennett drew his gun and swung toward Charlie Oliver.

"Shoot it," Oliver said. "What difference does it make? Shoot your gun. Kill me. Save everyone time and money."

"Sit down," Bennett said. "Over there, where I can watch you."

Charlie Oliver did as he was told. Bennett leaned forward, rolled Sonny over, and picked up the knife.

He pointed down at Sonny. "He always been this nutty?" he asked.

"Since he was a child," Oliver said, dully. "He's always lived in a rage. He was hospitalized for a while."

"What for?"

274

"Trying to murder his father," Charlie Oliver said.

"How long ago was that?" Bennett asked, looking down at Sonny, whose tightly drawn face smoldered with anger.

"He was ten years old," Charlie Oliver said. "Franny was the only one who visited him. He adores her. He'd do anything for Franny."

Bennett grunted. "It's too damn bad you people couldn't just kill each other and be done with it, instead of slaughtering a bunch of poor bastards who wouldn't harm a flea."

"They were throw-aways," Charlie Oliver whispered. "To accomplish your ends you sometimes have to get rid of a couple of throw-aways. What difference does that make? We're talking about love. About families. About the terrible things that sometimes happen to families." He looked up at the portrait of Gwen. "What does the death of a couple of throw-aways matter when you're talking about love?" he asked. He wiped his eyes with his hands and turned back to Bennett. "He took my child and used her and discarded her. It's only right that I did the same, I took his child and used him and discarded him," he said, touching Sonny with the toe of his shoe.

"Grandpa?" Eileen stood at the door, her eyes wide with fear. Behind her Franny held the child by the shoulders.

"You're supposed to be asleep," Charlie Oliver said, hurrying to the little girl. She tore herself loose from Franny's grip and grabbed her grandfather, hugging herself to him. "Grandpa," was all she was able to say.

Charlie Oliver looked up at Franny, his eyes asking if Eileen knew, if she'd heard. Franny nodded.

"I wish you'd been able to stay silent," Franny said. "I wrote a letter this afternoon, when I knew it would

275

be all over today, and I mailed it. Oh, my dear, I wish you'd been able to stay silent."

Charlie Oliver was stroking Eileen's head with his old, gnarled hand. He didn't understand Franny.

"I took the blame. I explained why I had killed everyone. I was going to take Sonny away with me, and you and Eileen would be together." For an instant her composure nearly shattered. She drew a deep shuddering breath. "Oh, my dear, if only you'd been able to stay silent."

"Thank you, love," Charlie Oliver said. "But it wasn't necessary." He looked over his granddaughter's head toward Gwen's portrait. "She's revenged," he said. "That's what was important, and I'm the only one who could do that."

23

Bennett drove back to the motel after he'd called Drang and told him to get some manpower to Charlie Oliver's house. He strutted when he stepped from his car. He had done it! He had damn well done just what he had said he would do. He had solved the damn case, he had shown the chief and everyone else. He felt good. Proud of himself.

In the room he poured a drink, then sat on the edge of the bed and phoned Polly. He could hardly wait to tell her. He tried to organize the words so that he wouldn't stumble over them. After the phone rang unanswered for more than a minute, he slowly hung up. He felt let down. But then he figured she was out shopping, although it was nearly ten o'clock at night. He would go over to the house and surprise her, he decided. She would be as pleased as he was.

The knock on the door startled him. He opened it to see Drang standing there.

"Can I come in?" Drang asked.

Bennett stepped back. Drang entered the room and sat uncomfortably on a straight-backed chair in front of the maple desk.

"Well," Bennett said. "Congratulations are in order,

277

right? It came out like I had a hunch it would. Chief Victor prepared to back and fill?"

"He's bringing charges," Drang said sourly.

Bennett was astounded.

"Charges?" he asked. "What charges? Against who?"

"He's had a unit going through your records," Drang explained. "They found fifty grand in your savings account."

Bennett blinked, suddenly cautious. "Who gave them permission to dig into my personal affairs?"

Drang shrugged. "They did it," he said. "The chief figures he can make a case that you've been taking bribes."

Bennett sat down on the edge of the bed. "I haven't been taking bribes," he said. "You know that better than anyone. Why would I take a bribe?"

"For money," Drang said. "Because you wanted a lot of money."

Bennett didn't bother to reply.

"Where'd the fifty grand come from?" Drang asked.

Bennett wondered when J. D. had made the deposit.

"I can't help you if you aren't honest with me," Drang said. "The chief's got a real bug in his bonnet about you. Too many people know you've been right and he's been wrong. He's accusing you of failing to obey orders, of insubordination, of every damn thing he can think of. Now he's found that bank account, it gives him his case."

"What's he going to do about it?" Bennett asked. His voice sounded strange in his ears, as though someone else had asked the question.

"He's going to pressure you to resign, or he's going to kick you off the force. He thinks you've set a bad example for the other officers."

"What do you think?" Bennett asked. "Do you think I've set a bad example?"

"I don't know," Drang said. "He has a point, you know. You can't have a department where everyone goes off half-cocked doing what they want to do. There must be discipline. It's tough, and it sounds crappy, but it's true."

Bennett nodded. He didn't agree, but he could understand the logic. Then, suddenly curious: "How'd you know I was here?"

"I called your house. Polly told me."

"When'd you call?"

"Half-hour ago. After we cleaned things up at Oliver's."

"What's going to happen to the little girl?" Bennett asked. He felt as though he was about to take a long trip and had to settle his affairs.

"Charlie Oliver had his lawyer there before I left. The lawyer's taking care of her."

"What about her father?" Bennett wanted to know. "The kid's got a father. Can't she live with her own father?"

"That's not our problem," Drang reminded him. "The court will have to decide what happens to the child."

"You know something?" Bennett asked rhetorically. "What's wrong in the world is everybody's been standing in line so damn long that by the time they get to the head of the line they've forgotten why they're there. They're afraid to step out and do anything on their own, because they've been in line too long." He looked at Drang to see if he understood.

"I don't know what the hell you're talking about," Drang said roughly. "I'm not in line. Never have been."

"Of course," Bennett said softly. "No, I wasn't being

279

specific. I wasn't talking about anyone in particular," he said. "Figure of speech. An exercise for the old brain. A pointless philosophical debate. With myself, I suppose." He nodded imperceptibly. He had been talking about himself, the gesture acknowledged. He was the one who had been in line too long.

Drang broke the silence. "You did a hell of a job," he said. "I can't condone the way you went about it, but it was one hell of a job."

"Thanks," Bennett said. He wondered why Polly had answered the phone when Drang had called, but hadn't answered his call. Then he realized what a ridiculous case he was making. "How would she know it was me?" he asked aloud.

Drang was puzzled.

"Did Polly say she was going out?" Bennett asked.

"No. This is none of my business," Drang began, embarrassed.

"Right. None of your business."

Drang plowed on. "But since you're staying in a motel and it was Polly who told me where you were, I have to assume something's not going well between the two of you, and I just want to say I'm sorry as hell if that's the fact. Anything I can do to help, please call me."

"Nothing that can't be worked out," Bennett said, wondering how the hell it could be worked out. Although now, if he wasn't going to be on the force any longer, perhaps he and Polly. . . .

"Where do I reach you?" Drang asked, standing.

"Here. My home away from home."

"I'll keep you posted about the internal investigation," Drang said. "I'd suggest you forego a hearing and take whatever they hand you. Unless you're prepared to tell them where that money came from."

"It's none of their business," Bennett said. He knew that J. D. would go through the roof if he heard that, but Bennett felt his own privacy, and J. D.'s, were a lot more important than the information the department wanted in order to soothe the chief's wounded ego.

Drang seemed to have read his thoughts. "It's not just the chief, Fred," he said. "You've disobeyed orders, you've traveled into other jurisdictions without proper clearance, you've generally done this whole thing bass ackwards. Don't you know that?"

"Sometimes it's the only way it can be done," Bennett said. "No matter." He opened the door to his room. It had begun to rain, a soft rain, a combination of mist and drizzle and a few drops which plunked onto the hoods of the cars parked outside.

"I'll be here if you need anything," he told Drang, who'd followed him to the door. "For a while, anyway. Who knows, I might take a trip around the world."

"With Polly?" Drang asked. "That would be good for both of you."

"Maybe," Bennett said. "And maybe it's time I got out by myself and figured out what I want to do with my life. I'm the only one who knows—right, Captain?"

Drang turned up his jacket collar and ran to his car. He slid in, started motor and windshield wipers, turned on his lights, and backed out. He tooted twice before he turned from the driveway into the street, and drove off. Bennett went back inside the room.

He was going to try Polly again but he didn't. He poured another drink and decided Fred Bennett had a lot going for him. Right now, on a rainy night, sitting alone in a motel room, he decided he would begin a new life.